STARTING CAREER IN CYBERSECURITY

Rafael Pluta / Anand Shinde

DevOM

Ireland | Poland |Dubai | India | USA

Dedication

"This book is dedicated to all current and aspiring cybersecurity professionals charting their path through this complex and ever-changing digital world. It honors your curiosity, determination, and commitment to protecting what matters most in our connected society. To those defending our digital frontiers — may your careers be guided by purpose, knowledge, and integrity. May this compass help you navigate each step of your journey with clarity and confidence."

With deep respect and gratitude,
Fellow Cybersecurity Explorers

Rafael / Anand

Preface

In today's rapidly evolving digital landscape, Cybersecurity has become a critical priority for organizations and individuals alike. Yet, for aspiring and even seasoned professionals, navigating a cybersecurity career can often feel like an overwhelming maze. With countless domains, tools, certifications, and job roles to explore, the question remains: Where do I begin, and how do I grow?

This book, Starting Career in Cybersecurity, was born from that very question. Its purpose is simple yet vital — to serve as your trusted guide throughout your cybersecurity career journey. Whether you are just starting, looking to pivot into the field, or aiming for executive leadership roles such as Chief Information Security Officer (CISO), this book offers practical insights and actionable advice tailored to your needs.

Grounded in five core domains — Security Principles, Business Continuity and Disaster Recovery, Incident Response, Access Controls, and Network Security — the book presents a comprehensive yet approachable framework. Each domain unpacks foundational concepts, essential tools, and strategic thinking required to thrive in the field. The structure of the book, reflected in its clear Table of Contents, allows you to chart your learning path. You can deep dive into a specific area of interest or methodically work through all domains to build a broad and versatile skill set.

Importantly, this is not a book of abstract theory. It emphasizes real-world applications, cross-domain exposure, and the integration of soft skills—communication, adaptability, and critical thinking— alongside technical expertise. Understanding your values and motivations is also encouraged, as it helps you align your career choices with what drives you every day.

A key companion to this book is the Certified in Cybersecurity (CC) certification offered by the globally respected ISC2 (isc2.org). Designed for individuals entering the field, this certification provides an excellent foundation in core cybersecurity principles. This book is structured to complement your preparation for the CC certification — making it an ideal resource to strengthen your understanding, boost your confidence, and help you stand out in a competitive job market. By aligning your learning journey with an industry-recognized credential like CC, you position yourself for accelerated growth and success in the cybersecurity profession.

You will also find a practical focus on entry-level roles, aligned with the CIA Triad and ISO 27001 principles, providing clarity for those just entering the cybersecurity world. For more advanced professionals, the book offers guidance on leadership competencies and preparing for strategic roles where business and security converge.

Above all, this book is a compass — adaptable to your unique journey and goals. As cybersecurity threats evolve, so too must your knowledge and ability to adapt and respond. With patience, persistence, and the insights shared in these pages, you will be equipped to navigate this dynamic career landscape with confidence and purpose.

About the Author

Rafael Pluta is a visionary business leader with over 15 years of expertise in IT and Cybersecurity for enterprise organizations. Throughout his distinguished career, he has successfully designed and implemented numerous strategies and security programs, including Security Operation Centers (SOC), Governance & Risk frameworks, Identity & Access Management (IAM), and Cloud Security initiatives. His trusted counsel has guided many C-level executives through complex security challenges.

Rafael holds an MBA in IT and multiple advanced certifications, including CCSP, CISSP, MISM, and AWS Architect. He has collaborated with leading Fortune 500 companies such as Citi Bank, 3M, Procter & Gamble, UBS, Capgemini, and Reckitt, consistently delivering impactful security solutions that mitigate risk and drive sustainable business growth.

His career is a testament to dedication and vision—beginning as an Infrastructure Engineer and advancing to the role of Group Director, giving him a comprehensive, hands-on understanding of the Cybersecurity domain. Rafael has built and led diverse, high-performing global teams across all regions, empowering employees and cultivating strong relationships with strategic partners and vendors.

A passionate advocate for innovation, Rafael actively explores the potential of AI and emerging technologies to enhance security capabilities and business operations. He believes in placing people at the heart of innovation and emphasizes the importance of continuous learning, collaboration, and creative problem-solving.

Through this book, Rafael shares his insights and experience to help individuals build meaningful careers in Cybersecurity. His aim is to inspire professionals at all levels to stay curious, embrace change, and pursue excellence in this dynamic and rapidly evolving field.

About the Author

Anand Shinde is a renowned, seasoned Cybersecurity expert, mentor, and author with a wealth of experience in safeguarding digital ecosystems, as a certified professional with credentials from global leaders like Microsoft, Cisco, Amazon, ISACA and the International Society of Automation. Anand has worked on complex cybersecurity projects across India, Poland, Ireland, and the United States. His international career has equipped him with diverse perspectives and practical insights to address intricate cybersecurity challenges effectively.

In addition to his consulting work, Anand is deeply committed to education and mentorship. Since 2015, he has been serving as a student mentor and career counsellor for prestigious institutions, including Novel Group of Institutes and MIT ADT University, guiding aspiring professionals toward successful careers in cybersecurity. His role as a mentor for the International Society of Automation reflects his dedication to fostering talent in the ever-evolving cyber landscape.

Anand has also contributed to the field of cybersecurity and artificial intelligence with an innovative patent application, underscoring his commitment to advancing the industry. His contributions extend to raising cyber awareness through blogs and campaigns that promote best practices for digital strength.

For anyone aspiring to build a career in cybersecurity, Anand invites you to connect through Devom, where he continues to empower individuals and organizations to thrive in the digital age.

TABLE OF CONTENTS

Introduction

How to Read This Book

Starting Career in Cybersecurity is designed to help you navigate your career path in the complex and ever-evolving world of Cybersecurity. Many aspiring professionals find themselves overwhelmed by the sheer number of available books, courses, certifications, and resources — not knowing where to begin or how to progress. This guide will serve as your personal compass — offering clear direction on what to do, how to do it, and how to build a strong foundation for your cybersecurity career.

To get the most out of this book, you can read it in two ways:

- If you have a target role or certification in mind, use the Table of Contents to focus on the most relevant domains and topics aligned with your goals.
- If you are exploring the field, or preparing for entry-level certifications like the Certified in Cybersecurity (CC) from ISC2, read through the entire book to gain a well-rounded understanding of core cybersecurity domains.

Importantly, this book is designed to complement one of the best starting points in the cybersecurity profession — the Certified in Cybersecurity (CC) certification offered by ISC2. ISC2 (International Information System Security Certification Consortium) is the world's leading cybersecurity professional organization, globally known for the prestigious Certified Information Systems Security Professional (CISSP) certification — widely regarded as one of the most respected and recognized certifications in cybersecurity. Earning a certification from ISC2 is a powerful way to establish your credibility as a cybersecurity professional.

Recognizing the growing demand for well-trained professionals, ISC2 launched the Certified in Cybersecurity (CC) course specifically for individuals serious about starting a career in cybersecurity — with no prior experience required. The best part? The CC exam is currently offered free by ISC2, making it an excellent and accessible first step into the field.

This book will help you prepare for the CC exam by providing a comprehensive overview of the key cybersecurity domains covered in the certification. Additionally, it will equip you with the mindset, soft skills, and technical foundation needed to succeed not only in the exam but in your career beyond.

You will explore five key domains: Security Principles, Business Continuity, Disaster Recovery, and Incident Response, Access Controls, Network Security, and Security Operations. Each domain unpacks essential concepts, tools, and practices required to thrive in the field. You'll also find guidance on entry-level roles aligned with the CIA Triad and ISO 27001 principles — giving you a practical understanding of real-world job opportunities.

Beyond technical knowledge, this book encourages you to reflect on your values, soft skills, and motivations. Cybersecurity is as much about people and mindset as it is about technology. A strong foundation in communication, problem-solving, and adaptability will serve you well as you progress.

Remember, building a career in cybersecurity takes time, dedication, and continuous learning. But with the right guidance — and by aligning your efforts with trusted certifications like those from ISC2 — your path becomes clearer and more achievable.

How to Proceed:

- Start by identifying your target role or certification goal (for example, preparing for the CC exam).
- Use this book to build foundational knowledge in all key domains.
- Focus on developing both technical and soft skills.
- Consider pursuing further certifications like CISSP as you progress.

Ultimately, to become a leader in cybersecurity — such as a CISO — you must develop expertise across all domains and continuously adapt to the changing landscape.

Take this book, chart your path, and begin your journey toward a rewarding career in cybersecurity.

Domain 1: Security Principles

Security principles are the fundamental concepts that underpin all cybersecurity efforts. These principles provide a framework for understanding and managing cybersecurity risks and for designing and implementing effective security controls. Security principles are important for all organizations, regardless of their size or industry sector. By following security principles, organizations can reduce the risk of cyberattacks and protect their data and systems. In the ever-evolving world of cyber security, a foundational understanding of core security principles remains paramount. These principles act as the bedrock upon which robust security frameworks are built, and they guide cybersecurity professionals in establishing defences against a variety of threats. Security principles advocate for a proactive, layered, and risk-based approach, ensuring that even if one line of defence is compromised, multiple layers work effectively to counteract potential cyber-attacks. Whether a seasoned professional or a newcomer to the field, understanding and adopting these principles is essential in our shared mission to safeguard the cyber world and organisations from cyber-attackers. Let us begin with understanding what cyber security really means.

1.1 What is Cyber Security?

In the 1950s, the word "Cyber" was used to refer to Cybernetics – The scientific study of control and communication between the animal and the machine. This was followed by "Cyber", standing for "computerized." The term Cyber security is disputed. The definition changes from one organization to another organization, from one nation to another nation. Even within a nation, the definition varies from one government department to the next. The Education Department may have a different definition than the Defense Division. This vagueness means it can cover an almost endless range of different issues, such as privacy or human rights. "A New America Foundation" study from 2014 found over 400 different Cyber Security definitions. Most of the definitions were developed over the years by research and development institutes, training institutes, Businesses, intelligence, and military actors focusing on the security of digital information and the network infrastructure that stores and transmits this information.

One might wonder why we are spending so much time talking about definitions. After all, it is just words, isn't it? Well, "The devil is in the detail". Small differences in the emphasis of Cybersecurity definitions can have big implications for human rights and actions. Definitions create the norms and rules on which policies are based and the narratives which justify them. If the definitions are too broad or focused on systems, they can be used to justify a wide range of measures, both legitimate and illegitimate.

Domain 1: Security Principles

Several bodies have helped to shape the International definition of Cyber Security. Technical bodies such as the Internet Engineering Task Force (IETF), The Internet Corporation for Assigned Names and Numbers (ICANN), and the International Telecommunications Union (ITU) are also active in developing their definitions of Cybersecurity. Broadly speaking, the widely accepted international definition as defined by ISO 27000 standards is "**Cyber-security** is the **Preservation through policy technology** and **Education** of the **Availability, Confidentiality,** and **Integrity** of **Information** and its **Underlying Infrastructure** to **Enhance** the **Security** of **Persons** both **Online** and **Offline**.

Understanding the differences between Information Security, IT Security, and Cybersecurity is essential for anyone working in or around the technology and security industry. Each has its scope, focus, and methods of operation, and while they may overlap, they are not identical.

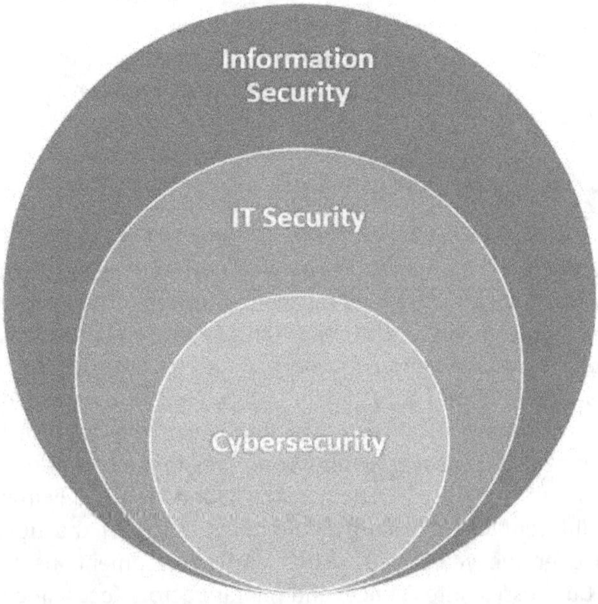

Let's start with Information Security, commonly referred to as InfoSec. This is the umbrella term under which all forms of data protection fall. Whether it's a physical document, an oral conversation, or digital data, InfoSec aims to safeguard all of this. The key principles are Confidentiality, Integrity, and Availability, collectively known as the CIA Triad. Confidentiality is about keeping secrets, well, secret. It ensures that information is only accessible to those who are authorized. Integrity means that the information remains unaltered and consistent, while Availability ensures that information is ready for use when needed. These principles apply whether you're securing physical files in a locked cabinet or encrypting digital files on a server. InfoSec leverages various controls, like physical measures (doors, locks), technical measures (firewalls, encryption), and administrative measures (policies, procedures), to achieve these goals.

Next, we have IT Security. If you think of Information Security as a large circle, IT Security would be a smaller circle within it. It deals explicitly with digital or technology-based assets, such as computers, servers, networks, and all the digital data that flows through them. The focus is still on the CIA Triad but within the digital realm. IT Security makes use of technical controls like firewalls, intrusion detection/prevention systems, and secure access controls to protect the digital environment. It's important to note that IT Security isn't just about keeping hackers out. It's also about maintaining system integrity and ensuring data availability. That means making sure software is updated to prevent potential vulnerabilities, ensuring hardware is robust and reliable, and having contingency plans like backups in place for data recovery.

Within the circle of IT Security exists Cybersecurity, an even more specialized field. It concerns itself only with networked, internet-connected assets. The primary threats here are from cyberspace – hackers, malware, phishing scams, ransomware, and the like. While IT Security covers all digital assets, whether they are networked or not, Cybersecurity is focused only on those digital assets that are connected to the internet. In Cybersecurity, there's a lot of talk about 'reducing the attack surface.' This means identifying and mitigating potential points of entry that attackers could exploit. For instance, if a company uses cloud-based servers, smartphones, laptops, and IoT devices, each of these becomes a part of the organization's ‘attack surface’. The larger the surface, the more effort is required to protect it.

At the intersection of these three fields are the elements of people, processes, and technology. Without well-trained people who understand the value of security, even the best technologies and processes can fail. Human errors or negligence often cause significant security breaches. Therefore, training and awareness programs are a must. Processes refer to the policies, procedures, and guidelines that govern how an organization approaches security. This can include everything from how often passwords must be changed to how data breaches should be responded to. Technology is the actual tools, hardware, and software solutions used to implement security measures.

In essence, all three fields aim to achieve the same core objectives of the CIA Triad but through different scopes and against different kinds of threats. Information Security is the broadest term that includes all types of information and means of protecting it. IT Security narrows this focus down to technological assets and digital information. Cybersecurity zeroes in on the protection of internet-connected systems and data from cyber threats.

So, to summarize, Information Security is the grand umbrella under which IT Security and Cybersecurity exist. IT Security covers all digital assets, while Cybersecurity focuses on those at risk of internet-based threats. Understanding the nuance between these can not only help in effectively communicating security needs but also in implementing the most effective security measures.

1.2 C I A Triad

To define Cyber Security one needs to have an understanding of the significance of the three foundational information security principles: Confidentiality, Integrity, and Availability, otherwise known as the ***CIA Triad***. The concept of the CIA triad formed over time and does not have a single creator. Confidentiality may have been first proposed as early as 1976 in a study by the U.S. Air Force. Likewise, the concept of integrity was explored in a 1987 paper titled "A Comparison of Commercial and Military Computer Security Policies." The paper recognized that commercial computing needed accounting records and data correctness. Even though it's not as easy to find an initial source, the concept of availability became more widespread one year later in 1988. By 1998 people saw the three concepts together as the CIA triad.

- **Confidentiality** – information is not disclosed to unauthorized individuals.
- **Integrity** – ensuring accuracy and completeness of data.
- **Availability** – users must have information when they need it.

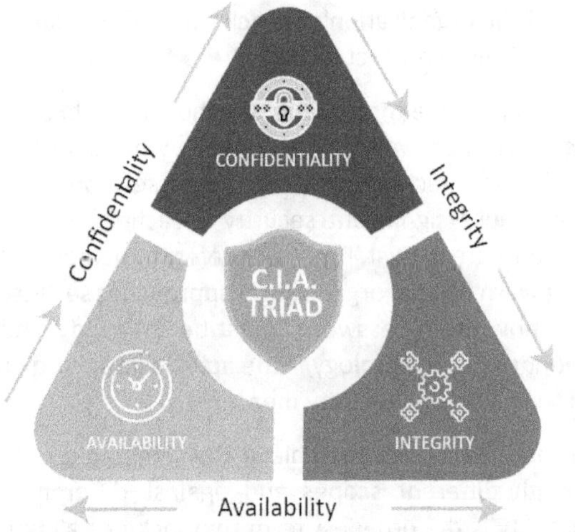

The CIA Triad is a central tenant of ISO/IEC 27001:2013 (ISO 27001), the international standard that describes best practices for an ISMS (information security management system). ISO 27001 neatly summarizes Information security as the maintenance of confidentially, availability, and integrity of the confidential assets of an organization

CIA Triad is a model designed to guide policies for information security. It provides us with a reference to evaluate and implement secure information systems, independently of the underlying technologies. Each one has specific requirements and processes. CIA Triad is aimed at protecting the organization's digital assets against ever-growing Cyber-attacks. This can be ensured by deploying appropriate security controls to provide several security features such as deterrent, prevention, and detection of Cyber-crimes. In this context, confidentiality is a set of rules that limits access to information, integrity is the assurance that the information is trustworthy and accurate, and availability is a guarantee of reliable access to the information by authorized people. Let us look at the components of the CIA Triad individually.

1.2.1 Confidentiality

Confidentiality is roughly equivalent to privacy. Confidentiality ensures the privacy of sensitive information while it is in transit over a network. Proactive measures undertaken to ensure confidentiality are designed to prevent sensitive information from unauthorized people/processes while making sure that only authorized people and only the intended parties have access to it. The malicious actors must not intercept the data to use it for nefarious purposes. It is common for data to be categorized according to the amount and type of damage that could be done should it becomes accessible to authorized people/processes. Various implementations can be incorporated to ensure the confidentiality of data. Safeguarding data confidentiality involves special training for those who need to access and work on sensitive data. This training would typically include an understanding of security risks that could compromise Confidentiality. Training can help users to get familiarize themselves with risk factors and how to safeguard against common attacks. Further aspects of training should include password-related best practices and information about social engineering methods, to prevent users from bending data-handling rules with good intentions and potentially disastrous results.

An example of a method used to ensure confidentiality is an account number or token number when banking online. Cryptography is the best solution in this regard. Data encryption is one of the most common and robust methods of ensuring confidentiality. Encryption mainly ensures the confidentiality of sensitive data. It converts the plaintext of data into Cipher-text, which is an unreadable form for humans. Cipher text can only be understood by authorized entities. Encryption might involve one of the two vital security controls either Symmetric Encryption or Asymmetric Encryption. User IDs and passwords constitute a standard procedure; two-factor authentication is also being implemented in most online banking transactions. Other options include biometric verification and security tokens, soft or hardware tokens. Users can also take precautions to minimize the number of places where the information appears and the number of times it is transmitted to complete a transaction. Extra measures might be taken in the case of extremely sensitive data, such as storing only on air-gapped computers and networks, and disconnected storage devices for highly sensitive information, in hard copy form. In addition, users can also use Steganography to hide data into another type of data such as images, audio, or video files. Hidden sensitive data in large media files is much more difficult to compromise.

Confidentiality should ensure that:

1. Data should be handled based on their required privacy.
2. Data should be encrypted, with a form of two-factor authentication to reach it.
3. Keeping access control lists and other file permissions up to date.

1.2.2 Integrity

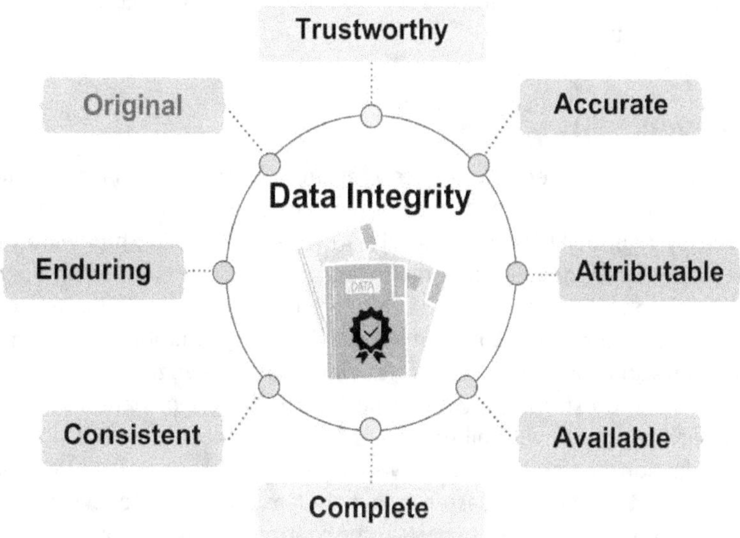

Integrity involves maintaining the consistency, accuracy, and trustworthiness of data over its entire life cycle. Integrity refers to preventing data from being tampered with, modified, or altered maliciously to achieve malicious goals. That means data that is sent must be received intact and unaltered by an authorized party. Data must not be changed in transit, and steps must be taken to ensure that data cannot be altered by unauthorized people (a breach of confidentiality). Integrity is essential for data whether it is in transit or it is in a storage media. Data integrity is crucial for E-commerce and business websites. These measures include file permissions and user access controls. Version control may be used to prevent erroneous changes or accidental deletion by authorized users from becoming a problem. Various attacks that compromise data integrity include a Man-In-the-Middle (MITM) attack, penetrating the web server, and introducing malicious code in databases.

In addition, some means must be in place to detect any changes in data that might occur as a result of non-human-caused events such as an electromagnetic pulse (EMP) or server crash. Use of Hashing Algorithms such as MD5 and SHA1 are normally provided by developers to check the integrity of data. Other techniques include certificates, digital signatures, and non-repudiation. Some data might include checksums, even cryptographic checksums, for verification of integrity. Backups or redundancies must be available to restore the affected data to its correct state.

Integrity should ensure that:

1. Employees are knowledgeable about compliance and regulatory requirements.

2. Use backup and recovery software.
3. To ensure integrity, make use of version control, access control, data logs, and checksums.

1.2.3 Availability

Availability is also a security service that ensures the constant availability of resources and services to only authorized parties on time. Availability is best ensured by rigorously maintaining all hardware, performing hardware repairs immediately when needed, and maintaining a correctly functioning operating system environment that is free of software conflicts. Reliable hardware must be maintained to provide constant services to a large number of customers in any organization. There must be less downtime during upgrades and backup of sensitive data in external drives will be helpful in case of data loss. It's also important to keep up with all necessary system upgrades. Providing adequate communication bandwidth and preventing the occurrence of bottlenecks are equally important. Quick disaster recovery plans should be followed in worst-case scenarios. Other important security controls for availability include data backup, patching, and redundant systems. Redundancy, failover, RAID even high-availability clusters can mitigate serious consequences when hardware issues occur.

Fast and adaptive disaster recovery is essential for the worst-case scenarios; that capacity is reliant on the existence of a comprehensive Disaster Recovery Plan (DRP). Redundancy ensures fault tolerance. It means, when a primary system fails to perform, the secondary system is available to continue the delivery of functions and services. In this case, security analysts redirect all traffic or workload to a backup system. Safeguards against data loss or interruptions in connections must include unpredictable events such as natural disasters and fire. To prevent data loss from such occurrences, a backup copy may be stored in a geographically-isolated location, perhaps even in a fireproof, waterproof safe. Extra security equipment or software such as firewalls and proxy servers can guard against downtime and unreachable data blocked by malicious denial-of-service (DoS) attacks and network intrusions.

Availability ensures that:

1. Use preventative measures such as redundancy, failover, and RAID. Ensure systems and applications stay updated.
2. Use network or server monitoring systems.
3. In case of data loss, ensure a Data Recovery and Business Continuity plan is in place.

1.3 Three Stages of Data

Understanding the three states of data is essential in the realm of cybersecurity. Based on the stage the data is at current stage, the security measures need to be deployed to ensure data protection. Every data stage offers its unique challenge and requirements for smooth data utilisation. Applying inappropriate data protection methods may affect the confidentiality, integrity or availability and may render the data useless or hinder the users' ability to access the data. Let us have a close look at the three stages of the data. Let us take a detailed look at these different parts.

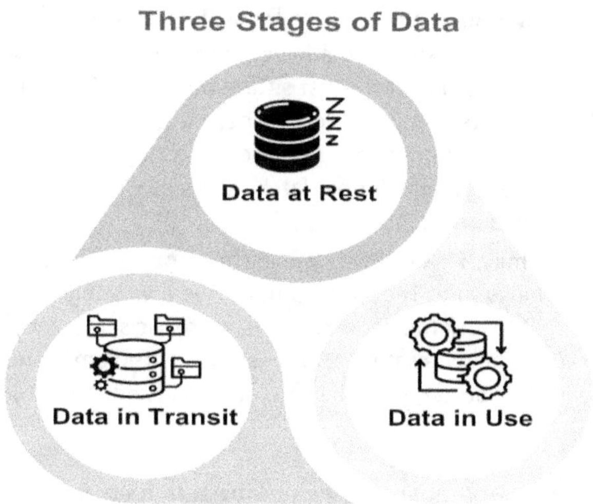

A) Data at Rest:

Protecting data at rest is like safeguarding a family treasure. Know what you have, decide how important it is, lock it up securely, make sure the environment is safe, and teach everyone the ground rules. That way, you're doing your best to keep those treasures safe.

1. **Know What and Where Your Data Is:** Imagine your company's data as your family jewellery; you would not just throw rings and necklaces in random drawers. First, you need to know what you have and where it is kept. In business, this means identifying which pieces of data are valuable or sensitive. It could be anything from customer emails to secret recipes. Once you know what you're dealing with, figure out where this data is stored. You cannot protect what you don't know exists.
2. **Label Your Data:** The next step is to decide how important each piece of data is. Think of it like sorting your jewellery into categories—daily wear, special occasions, and priceless heirlooms. In a business setting, this is called data classification. And just like styles change, the importance of data can too. So you have to keep reassessing. Maybe a piece of information that was just costume jewellery last year is a valuable antique this year. Update your security measures to match.
3. **Lock Up Your Treasures:** Now, would you leave your precious jewellery lying around? No, you lock it up. The same goes for data; you encrypt it. Encryption is like a digital lock and key for your data. Some people worry that these locks make it harder to access the data quickly (like fumbling with a tricky lock), but the added security is worth it. Not everything has to be locked up the same way; you might use a simple lock for less important things and a bank vault for the precious stuff.
4. **Make Sure the House is Secure:** Your jewellery is only as safe as the home it is in. So, you make sure doors have strong locks, and maybe even get a security system. Data at rest—just sitting there not doing anything—is the same. The computers and networks where it is stored need to be secure. This means regularly updating software to fix any vulnerabilities, just like you would fix a broken window latch, and always be on the lookout for burglars trying to break in.
5. **Train Your Family:** Finally, everyone in the family needs to know the basics of keeping things safe. They should not leave a valuable ring on the coffee table or forget to lock the door. Employees are the same; they need to know how to handle the data safely. A lot of security problems come from people not knowing any better, so make sure everyone knows the rules.

B) Data in Use:

Securing data in use or motion is like making sure a car is safe for a journey. Decide who should have the keys, equip the car with safety features like seat belts and airbags, and install a dashcam to monitor things. This way, you can be confident that your data is in safe hands and will reach its destination without any hitches.

1. **Choose Who Gets the Keys:** Imagine your data is like a fancy car. You would not just give the keys to anyone. Control who gets access to your data and make it specific. Instead of giving someone complete control of the car, maybe they only get a key to the trunk because that is all they need. In the digital world, this means allowing people to see only the parts of data they need for their jobs. It is like giving the valet a key that only starts the car but doesn't open the glove box. This makes sure that no one can accidentally leak information they shouldn't even be seeing in the first place.
2. **Use Seat Belts and Airbags for Your Data:** When you're driving, you put on a seatbelt, and your car has airbags to keep you safe in case of an accident. For data that's being used or sent somewhere, encryption is like those safety features. Always 'buckle up' your data when it's travelling, whether it's inside your company or going outside. Use trusted methods like HTTPS or SSL/TLS to create a 'protected lane' for it to travel safely. If it is precious data, consider even stronger protective measures like a VPN.
3. **Install a Dashcam to Monitor Activity:** These days, many cars have dashcams to record what's happening. It is an excellent way to spot any risky driving or accidents. When it comes to your data, having 'visibility' is like having a dashcam for your network. It helps you see who is doing what with your data. New innovative tools powered by Artificial Intelligence can analyse this 'footage' to spot anything odd. Maybe someone is trying to access data they shouldn't, or there's an unusual amount of data being sent out. These tools can alert you so that you can take action before anything terrible happens.

C) Data in Motion:

Now, let us say you have to transport your treasure chest to another place. You would want it to be secure while it is moving. That is what we call 'Data in Motion.' This is data that is being sent from one location to another, like emails or information accessed from web servers.

The goal is to ensure that nobody can intercept and understand the data while it is being transported. This is where 'end-to-end encryption' comes in. It's like sending your treasure chest in an armoured truck that can only be opened by the person at the receiving end. Even if someone manages to intercept the data, they cannot make sense of it without the decryption key.

1.4 IAAA Framework

The IAAA Framework is a cybersecurity framework developed by the Information Systems Audit and Control Association (ISACA). It provides a comprehensive and integrated approach to cybersecurity management.

The framework outlines the steps required to ensure that only legitimate user's access and interact with a system's resources, preserving its integrity and confidentiality. Identification introduces a user to the system. Once introduced, Authentication verifies the user's identity. After confirming legitimacy, Authorization dictates what actions the user is permitted to perform. Lastly, Accountability ensures that all actions are logged and traceable back to an authenticated entity.

The IAAA Framework is based on four pillars:

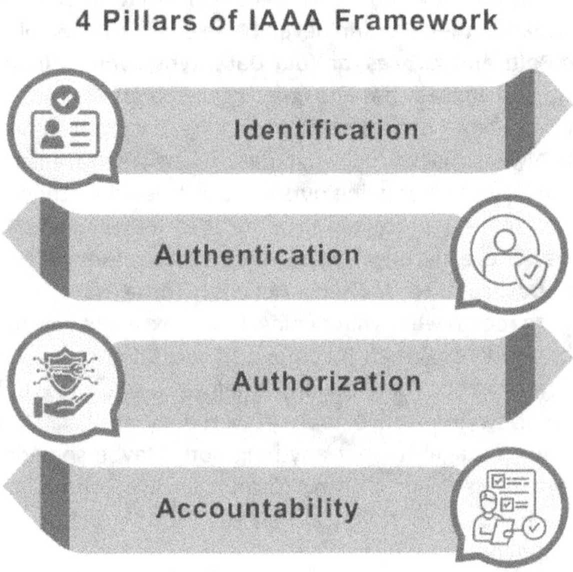

1. **Identification:** The Identify pillar focuses on identifying the organization's assets and the threats to those assets.
2. **Authentication:** The authentication pillar focuses on verifying the identity of users and devices.
3. **Authorization:** The Authorize pillar focuses on granting users and devices the appropriate access to assets.
4. **Accountability:** The Account pillar focuses on monitoring and auditing user and device activity to ensure that they are complying with security policies and procedures.

Let us look at the four pillars of IAAA framework in more detail.

1.4.1 Identification

Identification refers to a piece of information that distinguishes one entity from another. An entity could be anything from a person to a system process, and their unique identities allow the system to track and monitor who or what processes are carrying out which tasks. A common form of identity is a username, which is used in the authorisation process when you log in. Once logged in, your username can be used to track and identify your activity.

For the process of identification to function seamlessly and securely, several critical components must be in place:

1. **Unique Identity Assignment:** A robust system should be in place to generate and assign unique identities for each entity within the system. These identities should be specific to the domain or computer system in which they operate. This uniqueness is vital to prevent any overlap or confusion between entities.
2. **Mandatory Use of Identities:** To maintain the integrity of the identification process, entities must be compelled to use their assigned identities when accessing the system. Sharing identities should be strictly prohibited, as this could lead to unauthorized access and potential security breaches.
3. **Security Measures:** The identities themselves must be safeguarded through robust security measures. This includes secure storage of identity data, encryption to protect against eavesdropping, and continuous monitoring to detect any suspicious activities related to identities.

Identification plays a crucial role in auditing and accountability. It enables organizations to track who performed what actions within their systems. In case of security incidents or breaches, the ability to trace back to the responsible entity is instrumental in investigations, ensuring that appropriate actions are taken.

1.4.2 Authentication

Authentication is the process of recognizing a user's identity. It's the process of determining whether someone or something is who or what it declares itself to be. It is the mechanism of associating an incoming request with a set of identifying credentials. Authentication technology provides access control for systems by checking to see if a user's credentials match the credentials in a database of authorized users or a data authentication server. The credentials provided are compared to those on a file in a database of the authorized user's information on a local operating system or with an authentication server. Authentication is important because it enables organizations to keep their resources secure by permitting only authenticated users (or processes) to access their protected resources, which may include computer systems, networks, databases, websites, and other network-based applications or services. The process of determining claimed user identity by checking user-provided evidence is called authentication and the evidence which is provided by the user during the process of authentication is called a credential.

The authentication process always runs at the start of the application, before the permission and throttling checks occur, and before any other code is allowed to proceed. Different systems may require different types of credentials to ascertain a user's identity. The credential often takes the form of a password, which is a secret and known only to the individual and the system. Three categories in which someone may be authenticated are something the user knows, something the user is, and something the user has.

Once authenticated, a user or process is usually subjected to an authorization process as well, to determine whether the authenticated entity should be permitted access to a protected resource or system. A user can be authenticated but fail to be given access to a resource if that user was not granted permission to access it.

1. **How it is used:** User authentication is performed in almost all human-to-computer interactions other than guest and automatically logged-in accounts. Authentication authorizes human-to-machine interactions on

both wired and wireless networks to enable access to a network and Internet-connected systems and resources. Users are usually identified with a user ID, and authentication is accomplished when the user provides a credential, for example, a password, that matches that user ID. Most users are most familiar with using a password, which, as a piece of information that should be known only to the user, is called a knowledge authentication factor. Other authentication factors and how they are used for two-factor or multifactor authentication (MFA).

2. **How it works:** User authentication is the verification of an active human-to-machine transfer of credentials required for confirmation of a user's authenticity. User authentication is a security process that covers all of the human-to-computer interactions that require the user to register and log in. Said more simply, authentication asks each user, "Who are you?" and verifies their response.

When a user registers for an account, they must create a unique ID and key that will allow them to access their account later on. Generally, a username and password are used as the ID and key, but the credentials can include other forms of keys as well. To gain access, users must prove to the Authenticator that they are who they say they are. The ID and key are enough to confirm the user's identity, which will allow the system to authorize the user.

Generally speaking, authentication has three tasks:

- Manage the connection between the human (user) and the physical server (computer).
- Verify users' identities.
- Approve (or decline) the authentication so the system can move to authorize the user.

The process is fairly simple; users input their credentials. That information is then sent to the authentication server where the information is compared with all the user's credentials on file. When a match is found, the system will authenticate users and grant them access to their accounts. If a match isn't found, users will be prompted to re-enter their credentials and try again. After several unsuccessful attempts, the account may be flagged for suspicious activity or require alternative authentication methods such as a password reset or a one-time password.

However, the web's application protocols, HTTP and HTTPS, are stateless, meaning that strict authentication would require end users re-authenticate each time they access a resource using HTTPS. Rather than burden end users with that process for each interaction over the web, protected systems often rely on token-based authentication, in which authentication is performed once at the start of a session. The authenticating system issues a signed authentication token to the end-user application, and that token is appended to every request from the client.

A) Authentication Server:

An authentication server is an application that facilitates the authentication of an entity that attempts to access a network. Such an entity may be a human user or another server. An authentication server can reside in a dedicated computer, an Ethernet switch, an access point, or a network access server. An authentication server is a database that stores user credentials—username and password—and typically group and attribute information. When a user signs in to the host, the user specifies an authentication realm, which is associated with an authentication server. The system forwards the user's credentials to this authentication server to verify the user's identity.

An authentication server supports the most common authentication servers, including Windows NT Domain, Active Directory, RADIUS, LDAP, NIS, RSA ACE/Server, SAML Server, and eTrust SiteMinder. It enables organizations to create one or more local databases of users who are authenticated. The system is preconfigured with one local authentication server for users called "System Local." This predefined local authentication server is a system database that enables organizations to create user accounts for user authentication quickly. This ability provides flexibility for testing purposes and for providing third-party access by eliminating the need to create user accounts in an external authentication server.

Authentication is the process of determining whether someone or something is actually who or what it declares itself to be. When a potential subscriber accesses an authentication server, a username and password may be the only identifying data required. In a more sophisticated system called Kerberos, the subscriber must request and receive an encrypted security token that can be used to access a particular service. RADIUS (Remote Authentication Dial-In User Service) is a commonly used authentication method. TACACS+ (Terminal Access Controller Access Control System Plus) is similar to RADIUS but is used with Unix networks. RADIUS employs UDP (User Datagram Protocol), and TACACS+ employs TCP (Transmission Control Protocol).

B) Authentication Factors:

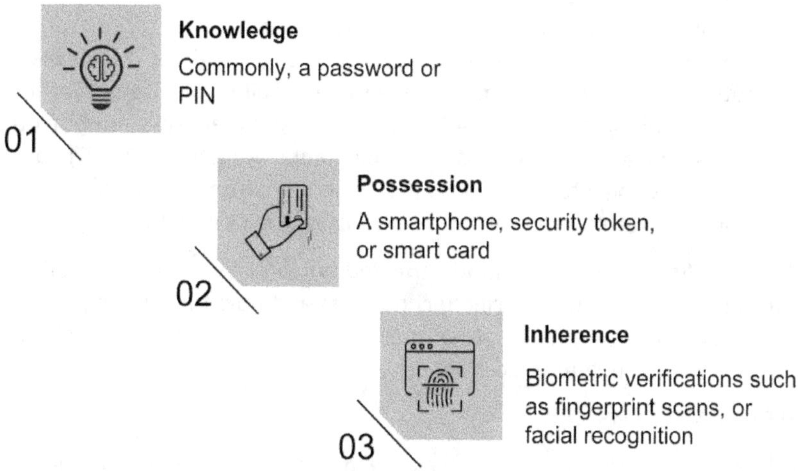

1. **Knowledge:** This factor includes all things a user must know to log in. User names, ID passwords, and PINs all fall under this category. To withdraw money from ATMs, the cardholder must know the card's PIN.
2. **Possession:** This factor consists of anything a user must have in their possession to log in; this category includes access cards, one-time password tokens, smartphone apps, employee ID cards, SIM card-based mobile phones, etc.
3. **Inherence:** This includes any inherent traits the user has that are confirmed to identity; this category includes a user's biometric features, such as Retina scans, Iris scans, Fingerprint scans, facial recognition, and voice recognition. Nowadays, these features are also present in most modern Cell Phones.

C) Supplemental Authentication Factors:

These three factors correspond to the knowledge factor, the possession factor, and the inherence factor. Additional factors have been proposed and put into use in recent years. Adding more than one authentication factor to the login or transaction typically improves security. The above three factors can be and sometimes manipulated. Additional factors which a Cyber attacker cannot manipulate can be introduced to improve authentication security. These factors are called Supplemental Authentication Factors. They are as below:

1. **Location:** User location is sometimes considered a fourth factor for authentication. Nowadays, most smartphones are equipped with GPS, enabling reasonable surety confirmation of the login location.
2. **Time**: This factor consists of "When a user is authenticating." Like the location factor, the time factor is not sufficient on its own. Still, it can be a supplemental mechanism for weeding out attackers who attempt to access a resource at a time when that resource is not available to the authorized user.

3. **Device:** In most organizations' users are given company assets, such as Laptops, desktops, Tablet PCs, Smartphones, etc. The users are expected to use these devices only to access the organizations' resources. The Authentication mechanism can be designed to allow the users to log in from these devices only. The MAC address / Physical address present on the assets can also be used as a Supplemental Authentication Factor. Any attempt to log into the Organization's network from any other asset other than the allotted asset can be blocked using the Device ID.

The reliability of authentication is affected not only by the number of factors involved but also by the specific technologies and how they are implemented. Well-designed and appropriately enforced implementation rules can help ensure the security of user authentication.

D) Single Sign On (SSO):

Although Authentication is a necessary process it is also important not to overburden users with complicated authentication routines, which can lead to non-compliance that undermines the purpose. Organizations also use authentication to control which users have access to corporate networks and resources, as well as to identify and control which machines and servers have access. Companies also use authentication to enable remote employees to access their applications and networks securely. But once logged in; the user may need to access various resources/services to do his work, such as Email, Instant messaging, file servers, print servers, Intranet, file servers, etc. Forcing a user to authenticate at every step can overwhelm and frustrate the user. To avoid this in large organizations, authentication may be accomplished using a single sign-on (SSO) system, which grants access to multiple systems with a single set of login credentials.

E) Single-Factor Authentication (SFA):

Single-factor authentication is the simplest form of authentication method. With SFA, a person matches one credential to verify himself or herself online. The most famous example of this would be a password (credential) to a username. Most verification today uses this type of authentication method. The traditional user authentication process for accessing computer resources. With single-factor authentication, only one category of credentials is specified, for example, username and password.

While single-factor authentication is commonly used in web emails, this Cybersecurity measure is also common as a perceived defensive measure in protecting endpoints—devices such as desktops and laptops that connect to a computer network and communicate with network resources.

One-factor authentication typically consists of passwords and passphrases, yet in recent years, it has also included biometric authentication. Most work-related activities, including emails and building access, are only set up for single-factor authentication, which isn't ideal as this tends to be the least secure option.

F) Risks of Single-factor Authentication:

The biggest challenge with the SFA is the password. Most of the users either don't understand how to make solid and memorable passwords or underestimate the need for security. There are two major mistakes users make which make Single-factor Authentication weaker than it inherently is. The first one is a **Simple Password**. Passwords are inherently flawed; users rely on memory; therefore, they will underestimate the need for higher security, choosing simple passwords that can be easily guessed or socially engineered. As computing power becomes increasingly available at affordable prices, attackers find it easier to break into accounts through brute-force methods, such as testing every possible combination in super-rapid succession to find the correct password. To avoid being brute-forced, users must choose passwords that are longer and more complex, containing lower- and upper-case letters, digits, and symbols. Users should also change their passwords regularly. This puts a lot of strain on users, especially when they must make the same considerations for dozens of online accounts. A lot of users avoid taking such measures. Year after year, studies find that such as "123456," "password" and other poor passwords remain extremely popular.

The second most common mistake users make is to reuse the same password across multiple accounts, which is also known as **Password Reuse.** One of the recommendations any cybersecurity expert will give is to avoid reusing passwords across multiple accounts. However, when users must maintain long and complex passwords across several accounts, they tend to reuse their passwords with minor or no variations at all. When hackers find the password to an account, they can quickly gain access to other accounts that use a similar password. Password-based security may be adequate to protect systems that don't require high levels of security, but even in those cases, constraints should be enforced to make them reasonably stringent. For any system that needs high security, more vital authentication methods should be used.

Single-factor authentication is not necessarily weak. Multiple challenge response questions can make for secure SFA authentication when adequately implemented. Many biometric authentication methods, for example, are vital when properly implemented. Biometrics can often make for secure SFA so long as the right kinds and implementations are chosen. Retina scans, finger vein scans, and voice recognition are good candidates. One must be doubly sure about the biometric scanner and its implementation when it is a standalone SFA solution rather than one component of MFA. Nowadays, many cell phone devices incorporate biometric authentication such as Fingerprint scans or Facial recognition. However, biometric verification systems may require a significant outlay for enterprise deployment. Depending on the degree of security required, it may be preferable to implement multifactor authentication.

G) Two-Factor Authentication (TFA):

Sometimes called 2-step verification or dual-factor authentication. Two-Factor Authentication is a security process to better protect users and resources by asking users to verify their identity in two ways. This process is done to protect better both the user's credentials and the resources the user can access. There are several ways to do this. The most common is a knowledge factor or something the user knows, like a password or PIN. Security question or some other shared secret. A possession factor is something the user has, such as an ID card, security token, or mobile device. An inherent factor or biometric factor is something physically inherent in the user like fingerprints or facial or voice recognition. Location factors and time factors are less common methods. Two-factor authentication requires two factors from two different categories. For example, a locked email account might ask security questions or knowledge factors and then send a code to a mobile device or another email account on record, a possession factor. Similarly, when facial recognition, a biometric factor, fails on users' mobile devices, it typically asks for a PIN code and not a fingerprint, which would be another biometric factor. Two-factor authentication is much more secure than single-factor authentication. Especially considering most single-factor services are password-based. Two-factor authentication provides a higher level of security than authentication methods that depend on single-factor authentication (SFA), in which the user provides only one factor - typically, a password or passcode.

Two-factor authentication adds a layer of security to the authentication process by making it harder for attackers to gain access to a person's devices or online accounts because knowing the victim's password alone is not enough to pass the authentication check. The vast majority of two-factor authentication methods rely on the three authentication factors. Knowledge, Possession, and inherence, though systems requiring greater security, may be them to implement multifactor authentication (MFA), which can rely on two or more independent credentials for more secure authentication.

H) Setting up Two-Factor Authentication:

The user needs to sign up / provide the necessary details to the authenticator before the Two-Factor authentication system can be activated. When a user signs up for two-factor authentication for a website or a service, a user generally provides his mobile phone number, which is one of the most common two-factor authentication modes used in general. If biometric systems are used in the two-factor authentication mode, then the user may be asked to scan his Retina, Iris, Fingerprint, and Face scan. Etc. These details are then stored in the Authentication Server for later use.

Most forms of two-factor authentication ask users to sign in with a username and password and then enter a code that is sent to their phone via SMS. Banking websites, shopping websites such as Amazon and Flipkart, and webmail services like Gmail use this method. This method not only proves that the user knows something (the username and password) but also that the user has something (the mobile phone) that the user has "registered" as a device to receive these codes.

1) How does two-factor authentication work?

Here is how the process breaks down step-by-step:

- The user is prompted to log in by the website or application.
- The user enters what they know, usually a traditional username and password combo. The site's server finds a match and recognizes the user. This step relies on the knowledge factor.
- For processes that don't require passwords, the website generates a unique security key for the user. The authentication tool processes the key, and the authentication server validates it.
- The site then prompts the user to initiate the second login step. Although this step can take some forms, users have to prove that they have something only they would have, such as a security token, ID card, smartphone, or other mobile device. This step relies on the possession factor.
- Then, the user enters a one-time code generated during step four. Some services use additional security measures, such as a time factor, where the user has to enter the password within 30 seconds or a minute. Failing to do so will take the user back to the first step.
- After providing both factors, the user is authenticated and granted access to the application or website.

2) Two-Factor Authentication Products: Most two-factor authentication solutions have multiple options, such as using hardware tokens, software tokens, or token-less authentication by utilizing SMS mobile phone technology. Two-factor authentication products can be divided into two categories: tokens that are given to users to use when logging in and infrastructure or software that recognizes and authenticates access for users who are using their tokens correctly. Authentication tokens may be A security token (or sometimes a hardware token, authentication token, USB token, cryptographic token, software token, virtual token, or key fob) may be a physical device that an authorized user of computer services is given to ease authentication. Examples are RSA Token and Symantec VIP Token.

3) Hard Tokens: A core feature of hard tokens is a screen for inputting and requesting access. This action can be done through an authentication code, biometric data, fingerprints, cryptographic keys, or a secure PIN. The types of tokens used can include USB tokens, Bluetooth tokens, smart cards, and more. In general, hard tokens are small and designed to be easily carried on a keychain or in a pocket or purse. Other types of hard tokens include connected tokens, which need a physical connection to automatically connect or transfer data and require host input services installed on the intended device. USB tokens and smart cards are commonly connected tokens that are still popular today. Disconnected tokens are the most common types of hard tokens. They require two-factor authentication, usually including a PIN, before allowing access. While disconnected tokens don't need to be plugged into their intended device, authentication is manually entered through a small screen on the token itself.

4) Soft Tokens: Soft tokens don't so much have "types" in the same sense as hard tokens, as they perform a variety of authentication options based on the program or app organizations choose for their authentication method. This process usually incorporates two or more steps to ensure maximum security. It can include one-time passwords that last a limited time (often associated with RSA SecurID soft tokens, which allow for approximately one minute before generating a new one-time password to use). Authentication codes can also be sent to users' smartphones or other connected devices or even use biometric data. While hardware-based systems are more secure, they are also costly and difficult to deploy on a large scale. A smartphone soft token app performs the same task as a hardware-based security token. Like a hardware token, a smartphone provides an easy-to-protect and easy-to-remember location for secure login information on the device itself. Unlike a hardware token, smartphones are connected devices, which makes them inherently less secure. Examples of Software Tokens are Microsoft Authenticator, Symantec Validation and ID Protection Service (VIP), CA Strong Authentication, Okta Verify, etc.

5) Hard vs Soft Tokens: Hard tokens, while considered incredibly secure, do have their downsides. Carrying a minor physical "key" for access can lead to problems if it gets lost, for example. Also, hardware token batteries have a limited life and cannot be recharged, with the typical lifespan being between three and five years. For small businesses, this expense can add up: after all, hard tokens, being physical objects, are a monetary investment in terms of their procurement. Soft tokens have some benefits and drawbacks worth considering as well. Soft tokens tend to rely on apps on devices such as smartphones to work, so users have to make sure to always have their phones with them when they want to use these devices. Smartphone batteries tend to die much faster than hard-token batteries. Another consideration is the price. While hard tokens have come a long way in both convenience and security, they're an investment and may not be the most convenient for small businesses. However, that price gets organizations high-quality security and reliability without the security concerns of hacked devices or compromised software. Soft tokens, on the other hand, are usually free to use and compensate for potential security issues through multi-factor authentication methods that are often time-based.

When choosing the "Type" of token, one has several considerations to keep in mind: price, ease of use, and confidentiality. For little to no cost, a simple SMS authentication or RSA soft token is the way to go, especially if there's not much need for securing private data. However, suppose the need for the security of confidential information is high. In that case, contactless hard tokens are easily the best bet, as they do not store any of the user's data and are not subject to hacking. If organizations are considering the use of biometric information in security tokens, then that is quite costly to implement, though worth it if the organization handles susceptible information. In many cases, two-factor authentication is a reliable solution for accessing software as needed. However, in case one or both authentication factors are compromised, a hard token backup is very secure and reliable.

I) Multi-Factor Authentication:

Multi-factor authentication is mainly used in businesses and government agencies that require high degrees of security. For a system to be considered multi-factor authentication, it is required that at least one element from each category be used. It is important to know that the reliability of authentication is affected not only by the number of factors involved but also by how they are implemented.

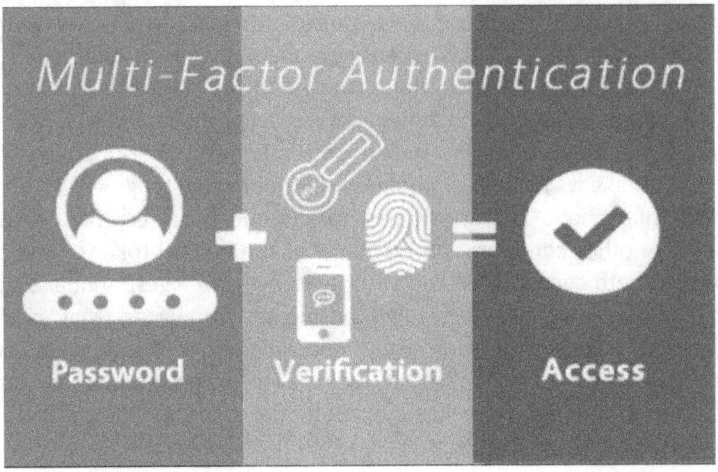

The factors include the following:

- Something the user is – Fingerprint, Retina or Iris Scan, Face recognition, voice recognition.
- Something the user has – Hard Token, Access / Smart card, USB Authentication token.
- Something users know – Password, PIN.
- Something users do – Signature, handwriting pattern, wipe strokes on a cell phone,
- Somewhere the user is – Location (GPS), Time-zone

Multi-factor authentication, or MFA, is an approach to protecting users' login credentials that requires the presence of two or more of the three independent authentication factors. A knowledge factor- something only the user knows. A possession factor - something only the user has. And an Inherence is something only the user is. The most popular form of multi-factor authentication is two-factor authentication, which is used by online services like Gmail, Steam, and Amazon. The three factors are pretty clearly defined. Knowledge factors include pin codes, personal questions like users' mother's maiden name, passwords, and swipe tap or lock patterns like those on smartphone lock screens. Possession factors are physical items like an identification card that one would swipe to access secure areas of a building or a USB Drive with an encryption key on it that decrypts the protected folder on a computer. Though for the most part possession factors are being eliminated and replaced by smartphone features and apps. Making users smartphone users possess factor. Inherence factors are also known as biometric identifiers. There are relatively new forms of authentication, including face recognition, fingerprint scans, voice prints, and Iris and retinal scans.

Now, there is no doubt that biometric authentication factors are very robust and quickly being pushed into the mainstream; they're also meeting a fair bit of resistance, and for good reason. One issue is that biometric information can be easily repeated once compromised. The second reason is that many individuals object to having their biometric information tracked and stored in a database. This seems like a reasonably valid concern, given the amount of secure data that gets compromised daily. Unlike a password, users cannot run around changing their fingerprints, retinas, or other biometric features.

Logging in by combining a knowledge factor like a password with a possession factor like a physical key or a code sent to a smartphone makes the account much more difficult to target for online attacks. Let us think of Gmail's two-factor authentication as an example. Suppose a Cyber Criminal obtains a user's password with a key logger or a security question exploit. In that case, Google will require the entry of a six-digit code that they send to the user that must be entered within a couple of minutes. Something that the hijacker can't get without the user's smartphone. On top of that, if someone tries to log in with the correct password, that notification will go straight to the user, and the user will immediately know that someone is trying to access his/her account without permission.

J) Authentication vs Authorization:

Although both terms sound similar, they refer to entirely different security processes. In the scope of customer identity and access management (CIAM), authentication verifies a user's identity, while authorization validates whether the user has access to perform a specific function. Authentication identifies users by confirming who they say they are, while authorization establishes a user's rights and privileges. Both processes play equally important roles in securing sensitive data assets from breaches and unauthorized access.

1.4.3 Authorization

Authorization happens after a user's identity has been successfully authenticated. It is about offering full or partial access rights to resources like databases, network resources, and other critical information to get the work done. In an organization, for example, after an employee is verified and confirmed via ID and password authentication, the next step would be defining what resources the employee would have access to.

Authorization Techniques:

1. **Role-based Access Controls (RBAC)** can be implemented for system-to-system and user-to-system privilege management. RBAC assigns roles to users or entities, and permissions are associated with these roles. Users are granted access based on their roles, simplifying permission management.
2. **Attribute-Based Access Control (ABAC):** ABAC evaluates access decisions based on attributes, such as user attributes, resource attributes, and environmental conditions, allowing for more fine-grained access control.
3. **Discretionary Access Control (DAC):** DAC allows resource owners to set access permissions for their resources. Users have some control over who can access their resources, making it flexible but potentially less secure.
4. **Location-Based Access Control:** Access is restricted or granted based on the user or device's physical or network location. This is particularly important in mobile and remote work environments.
5. **Mandatory Access Control (MAC):** MAC enforces access controls based on security labels and predefined security policies. It is commonly used in government and military settings.
6. **Rule-Based Access Control (RBAC):** RBAC uses rules to determine access permissions. Administrators typically define these rules and can be based on various conditions and criteria.
7. **Time-Based Access Control:** This technique restricts access based on specific periods or schedules. Users may only have access during designated times.

8. **JSON web token (JWT)** is an open standard for securely transmitting data between parties. Users are authorized using a public/private key pair.
9. **SAML** (Security Assurance Markup Language) is a standard Single Sign-On format (SSO) in which authentication information is exchanged through digitally signed XML documents.
10. **OpenID Authorization** verifies user identity based on an authorization server's authentication.
11. **OAuth** allows the API to authenticate and access the requested system or resource.
12. **Hierarchical Access Control:** Access permissions are determined based on an individual's position within an organizational hierarchy. Higher-ranking individuals may have broader access.

1.4.4 Accountability

Accountability is the fourth and final pillar of the IAAA Framework. It is essential to ensure that individuals and systems are accountable for their actions and that security controls are adequate. Organizations and individuals alike rely on digital systems to safeguard sensitive information, and this trust hinges on the assurance that actions taken within these systems are not only authorized but also traceable to their sources. This is where the "A" in the IAAA Framework, Accountability, comes into play. It refers to the concept of tracking and documenting all actions and events that occur within a system, especially those involving sensitive data or critical operations. The goal is simple but crucial: to establish a clear record of who did what, when, and why.

1.5 Non-Repudiation

Non-repudiation, in simple terms, means that once someone says or did something, they cannot deny it later. This is a cybersecurity concept that aims to prevent individuals or entities from denying the authenticity or integrity of a digital message, transaction, or action they were involved in. It assures that the sender of data cannot later disown their actions, and the recipient cannot refute receiving the data. Two primary facets of non-repudiation are:

1. **Proof of Origin:** Assures that a message's origin is genuine and can be verified.
2. **Proof of Delivery:** Confirms that a message was received by the intended recipient.

In this digital world, we use digital signatures, much like signing a letter, to prove that we sent a message or file. You sign it with your private key, which is like your secret code. This signature shows that you are the sender, and the message has not changed during transmission. Importantly, you do not encrypt the whole message, just this signature. When others receive your message, they use your public key, which is like a key to check your signature. They do not need your secret code (private key) for this. If the signature matches, it proves you sent the message.

Critical elements of non-repudiation include:

1. **Authentication:** Verifying the identity of the sender and receiver of data.
2. **Integrity:** Ensuring that the data has not been altered during transmission.
3. **Timestamping:** Providing proof of when a message or transaction occurred.
4. **Digital Signatures:** Using cryptographic techniques to sign data and verify its origin.

Non-repudiation is a vital cybersecurity concept that can help protect businesses and individuals from fraud and other malicious activity. Following are a few reasons

1. **Legal and Compliance Requirements:** Non-repudiation is crucial for legal purposes, as it provides evidence that can be used in disputes, contracts, and regulatory compliance. In many jurisdictions, digital signatures with non-repudiation hold the same legal weight as physical signatures.
2. **Dispute Resolution:** In cases of disputes, non-repudiation ensures that parties cannot deny their involvement in a transaction or communication. This reduces the likelihood of costly legal battles.
3. **Accountability:** Non-repudiation promotes accountability in both personal and business transactions. Knowing that actions cannot be denied encourages responsible behaviour in the digital realm.
4. **Data Integrity:** Ensuring data integrity and non-repudiation safeguards against data tampering ensures that information remains accurate and trustworthy.
5. **Security and Trust:** In a world where digital interactions are the norm, non-repudiation enhances security and builds trust among users, customers, and partners.

Non-repudiation is like a fundamental building block for trust in the digital world. As we do more and more things online and not in person, it is really important to be sure that what people do or say online is accurate and true. Non-repudiation helps make sure of this by making it impossible for someone to deny that they did something online or said something in a message. It's like a guiding light that makes sure our online world is trustworthy, genuine, and safe.

1.6 Privacy

Privacy is the fundamental right to control one's personal information and limit its access by others. In the context of cybersecurity, privacy goes hand-in-hand with security, as it encompasses the protection of sensitive data from unauthorized access, disclosure, or misuse. In today's digital era, as our lives become increasingly interconnected and digitized, the concept of privacy has taken centre stage. From personal details shared on social media to financial information exchanged during e-commerce transactions, the digital footprints we leave behind are vast.

Privacy is important for a number of reasons, including:

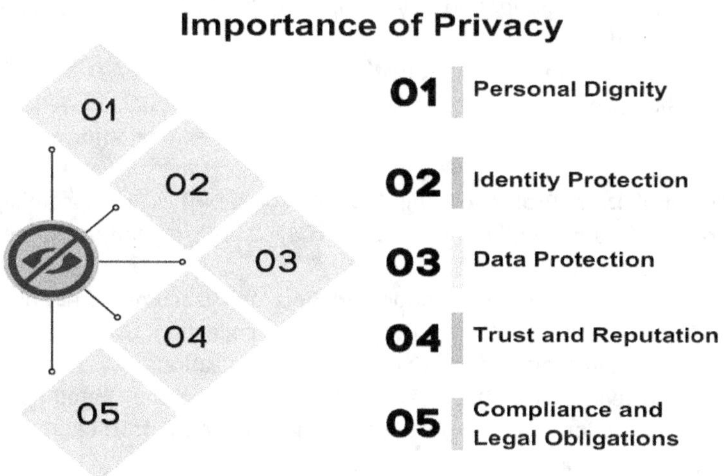

1. **Personal Dignity:** Privacy ensures that individuals can maintain their dignity by controlling what information about themselves is shared and with whom.
2. **Identity Protection:** It safeguards against identity theft and fraud, preventing malicious actors from misusing personal data for financial gain or impersonation.
3. **Data Protection:** Privacy is essential for protecting sensitive data such as financial records, medical history, and personal correspondence from unauthorized access.
4. **Trust and Reputation:** Organizations that prioritize privacy earn the trust of their customers and partners, enhancing their reputation and competitiveness.

5. **Compliance and Legal Obligations:** Many regions and industries have strict privacy laws that mandate the protection of personal information. Compliance is not just a legal obligation but also a matter of trust and integrity.

As the importance of privacy became universally recognized, governments worldwide have enacted regulations to safeguard individual data rights. Here's a brief overview of some key regulations:

1. **General Data Protection Regulation (GDPR):** GDPR is a European Union regulation that sets strict standards for the protection of personal data. It applies to any organization that processes the data of EU residents, regardless of the organization's location.
2. **California Consumer Privacy Act (CCPA):** CCPA is a California state law that grants California residents certain rights regarding their data, including the right to access and delete their information.
3. **Health Insurance Portability and Accountability Act (HIPAA):** HIPAA is a federal law in the United States that regulates the protection of medical information and patient privacy. It applies to healthcare providers, insurers, and related entities.
4. **Children's Online Privacy Protection Act (COPPA):** COPPA is a U.S. federal law that protects the online privacy of children under 13 years old. It requires parental consent for the collection of personal information from minors.
5. **Personal Data Protection Bill (PDPB):** The PDPB is an upcoming data protection law in India that will govern the collection and use of personal data in the country.
6. **Personal Information Protection and Electronic Documents Act (PIPEDA):** PIPEDA is a Canadian law that regulates the collection, use, and disclosure of personal information by private-sector organizations.
7. **Data Protection Act 2018 (DPA 2018):** DPA 2018 is the United Kingdom's implementation of GDPR post-Brexit. It governs data protection in the UK and applies similar principles to GDPR.
8. **Privacy Shield:** While not a law, Privacy Shield was an agreement between the EU and the U.S. that facilitated data transfers between the two regions while ensuring that European data privacy standards were upheld.
9. **Brazilian General Data Protection Law (LGPD):** The LGPD is a Brazilian data protection law that governs the processing of personal data in Brazil and applies to any organization handling Brazilian data.
10. **Digital Personal Data Protection Act (DPDP2023):** Data Protection Board of India (DP Board)—to oversee compliance, impose penalties, address data breaches, conduct investigations, and resolve grievances. The DPDP also establishes a framework for the processing of personal data by businesses and other organizations, including consent requirements, data localization requirements, and data subject rights.

Privacy is a fundamental human right essential for personal autonomy and dignity. Organizations have a responsibility to protect the privacy of their customers and employees. By following the best practices outlined in this chapter, organizations can help protect privacy and build trust with their stakeholders.

1.7 Understand the Risk Management Process

Most organizations do face many risks. Examples include cyber-attacks, data breaches, operational disruptions, system failures, economic or political crises, and natural disasters. With an effective risk management process, a company can identify which of these risks pose the biggest threats and then implement the best measures to those risks at acceptable levels. A reliable risk management process and a detailed risk management plan can help you understand and control risk.

This risk management process consists of a series of steps or activities. Here Are The Five Essential Steps of A Risk Management Process:

A) Step 1- Risk Identification:

The first step of risk management is to identify the risks that the business has discovered in its operating environment. There are many types of risks, including legal risks, environmental risks, market risks, regulatory risks and much more. It is essential to identify as many of these risk factors as possible. If the organization has employed a risk management solution, all this information is included directly in the system. The advantage of this strategy is that these risks are now transparent to every stakeholder in the organization with access to the system.

In the risk management process, the first step is risk identification. This step involves detecting and listing all potential risks that could affect the organization's assets and critical business processes. This process aims to identify any risks that might impact its performance, operations, or reputation. Here's how the risk identification process unfolds:

1. **Identifying Information Assets**: It all starts with recognizing the company's information assets and understanding their value to the organization. These assets can be physical, like computers and facilities, or intangible, like reputation, data, and intellectual property. Knowing their value helps determine the necessary security measures and allocation of funds.

2. **Determining Threats**: The next step is to determine what threats could target these assets and where they come from. There are three primary sources of threats: internal (like human errors or employees revealing sensitive information), external (like hacking or natural disasters), and emerging (new or recently introduced risks).

3. **Identifying Vulnerabilities**: Vulnerability identification involves finding security weaknesses in a company's systems, infrastructure, and applications. Techniques like vulnerability scanning, penetration testing, security audits, and code reviews help identify these weaknesses.

It is important to note that risk identification is not a one-time task. Risks can evolve, and new ones can emerge over time. Therefore, it should be an ongoing process throughout the project, program, or organization being assessed for risk to ensure continued protection and preparedness.

B) Step 2 - Risk Analysis:

After identifying a risk, the next step is to analyze it. This involves understanding its size and how it might affect various parts of the organization. To assess how severe a risk is, we need to see how many different parts of the business it affects. Some risks could potentially bring the entire business to a halt if they actually happen, while others might only cause minor inconveniences.

1. **Analyzing Security Controls:** In this step, you evaluate how effective the existing security measures are in reducing the risk impact. This analysis reveals any shortcomings or areas that need improvement to address the risk.
2. **Determining Loss Potential**: Loss potential means understanding what the company could lose if a threat actually exploits a vulnerability. This loss could involve data corruption, system destruction, unauthorized data disclosure, reduced employee productivity, and more. Factors like the type

of vulnerability, threat source capabilities, and security control effectiveness are considered when assessing consequences.

3. **Using Different Techniques**: Various techniques, such as historical analysis (looking at past security events), systematic examination (scrutinizing business processes for potential failures), and inductive analysis (identifying specific points of attack), can help identify risks.

In a manual risk management setup, this analysis has to be done by people. But when risk management software is used, one of the most important steps is to link risks to different documents, policies, procedures, and business processes. This means the system already has a framework for evaluating risks and can show how widespread each risk's impact might be. It makes it much easier to understand the potential consequences of different risks and plan accordingly.

C) Step 3- Risk Assessment:

Risks have to be sorted and ranked in order of importance. In most risk management systems, risks are divided into categories based on their severity. Risks that might cause minor issues get a low rating, while those that could lead to massive losses get the highest rating.

This ranking process is essential because it gives the organization a complete picture of how exposed it is to risks. There might be many small risks that don't need top-level management attention. But even just one of the highest-rated risks can demand immediate action because of the potentially severe consequences it carries. So, by prioritizing risks, organizations can focus their efforts where they are most needed and ensure that critical risks are addressed promptly. There are two types of risk assessments: Qualitative Risk Assessment and Quantitative Risk Assessment.

1. **Quantitative Analysis:** Quantitative analysis plays a crucial role in risk assessment. This involves evaluating the likelihood of specific threats impacting the organization. Key calculations include the Annualized Rate of Occurrence (ARO) and the Single Loss Expectancy (SLE). The ARO indicates the probability of a particular threat happening within a year. It is important to adjust this calculation based on the organization's geographical location and unique circumstances. The SLE, on the other hand, measures the cost associated with a single adverse event. For example, if a laptop is stolen, the SLE would be the cost of replacing it, say $1,000. To determine the potential annual loss, multiply the ARO by the SLE, resulting in the Annual Loss Expectancy (ALE). For example, if the estimated ARO is seven laptop thefts per year, the ALE would be $7,000.

2. **Qualitative Risk Analysis:** Risk assessments are inherently qualitative—while we can derive metrics from the risks, most risks are not easily quantifiable. For example, the risk of climate change that many businesses are now focusing on cannot be fully quantified; only different aspects of it

can be measured. There needs to be a way to perform qualitative risk assessments while still ensuring objectivity and standardization across the enterprise. Qualitative risk analysis offers a framework to evaluate risks based on various factors, including impact, ARO, cost of controls, and overall risk value. These factors are often scored or categorized on a scale from 1 to 10 or using a traffic light system (red, yellow, or green) to assess risk severity.

D) Step 4 - Risk Treatment:

When it comes to managing risks, the goal is to either eliminate them or minimize their impact as much as possible. To achieve this, it is crucial to collaborate with experts in the specific field related to the risk. In a manual setup, this collaboration involves reaching out to each stakeholder individually, setting up meetings, and having discussions. However, this can become quite chaotic. Conversations are scattered across multiple email threads, various documents and spreadsheets, and numerous phone calls.

On the other hand, with a risk management solution, things become much more streamlined. You can notify all the relevant stakeholders directly from within the system. Discussions about the risks and potential solutions can happen within the system itself. Upper management can closely monitor the suggestions and track the progress, all from the same platform. Instead of constantly reaching out to one another for updates, everyone can access the latest information and updates directly from the risk management solution. This simplifies communication and ensures that everyone involved is on the same page, making the process of managing risks more efficient and effective.

E) Step 5- Risk Review & Monitoring:

Not all risks can be avoided entirely or eliminated; some risks are always there. Market dangers and environmental dangers are examples of risks that are always around. In old-fashioned systems, people have to watch out for these risks carefully. These experts need to keep a very close eye on everything that might go wrong.

But when we use a digital system, it looks out for risks all by itself. It keeps an eye on all the risks that an organisation might face. If anything changes, everybody can see it right away. Computers are much better at doing this job all the time compared to people. Monitoring risks also helps a business stay running smoothly.

1.8 Understand Security Controls

Security controls are safeguards or countermeasures that are implemented to protect information and systems from unauthorized access, use, disclosure, disruption, modification, or destruction. Security control is an organisation's parameter and action to protect data and sensitive information from invasion and various cyber-attacks and reduce and mitigate existing security risks or threats on critical assets (i.e., data, system, network or cloud risks). Security controls can be technical, administrative, or physical. Antivirus software, Host-based IDS, SIEM solutions, hardware or software firewalls, surveillance systems, security guards, smart door locks, and CASB security for the cloud are some of the significant examples of security controls.

A) Purpose:

Appropriate cyber security controls are fundamental to reducing the outcome and probability of cyber security incidents. In addition, information or cyber security controls help ensure that all the necessary and required actions are in place to hold the business's proprietary information's CIA triad. Security controls are not chosen or implemented arbitrarily. They typically flow out of an organization's risk management process, which begins with defining the overall IT security strategy and goals. This is followed by defining specific control objectives—statements about how the organization plans to manage risk effectively.

B) Types of security controls:

There are three main types of security controls:

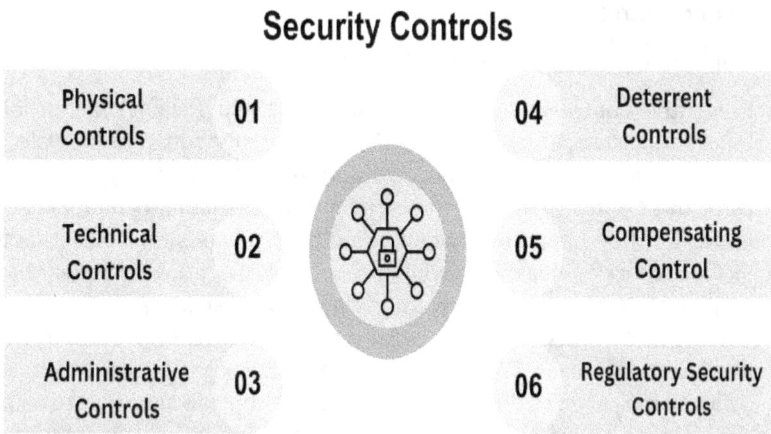

1. **Physical controls:** Physical controls are physical measures that are implemented to protect information and systems from physical threats. Examples of physical controls include access control systems, security cameras, and environmental controls.
2. **Technical Controls:** Technical controls are implemented using hardware, software, and firmware. Examples of Technical controls are Firewalls, Intrusion detection systems, Encryption, Antivirus software, Data loss prevention systems, and Access control systems.

3. **Administrative controls:** Administrative controls are policies and procedures that are implemented to manage the security of information and systems. Examples of administrative controls include security awareness training, background checks, Incident response plans, Password policies, Data classification policies, etc.
4. **Deterrent Controls:** Deterrent controls aim to lower the chances of a deliberate attack and typically involve a physical object or person. Their purpose is to dissuade individuals from engaging in actions that could lead to an incident.
5. **Compensating Control:** Compensating controls are security measures employed temporarily to meet required security standards or decrease business risk. These controls are often used when facing financial constraints, complex infrastructure, impractical implementation, or limited time for remediation.
6. **Regulatory Security Controls:** Regulatory controls are security measures mandated by legal and regulatory bodies like PCI-DSS, GDPR, HIPAA, and ISO 27001 to ensure compliance. These controls involve implementing organizational policies that address data security, protection, individual privacy, security awareness, and cyber assessments in accordance with regulatory requirements.

C) Security Control Mode:

There are three primary modes of security control:

1. **Preventive Controls:** These are measures that help prevent cyber problems before they start. They include antivirus programs, software firewalls, and blocking bad internet traffic or unauthorized access.
2. **Detective Controls:** These are security measures that find and report cyber issues as they happen or when something seems suspicious. Examples include checking logs, receiving security alerts, using intruder alarms, employing SIEM solutions, and using video surveillance.
3. **Corrective Controls:** These are security measures that organizations should already have in place. They involve actions and plans to lessen the impact of a data breach or any cyber incident. Corrective controls are a way to respond and recover, helping the business keep running with as little downtime as possible. Examples of corrective security controls include having an incident response plan and backups.

1.9 Understand the ISC2 Code of Ethics

The International Information System Security Certification Consortium is popularly known as ISC^2 or ISC2. This is a non-profit organization which specializes in training and certifications for cybersecurity professionals. As of today, the society has 500,000 members worldwide. ISC2 has long been recognized as a global leader in certifying and nurturing cybersecurity professionals. Central to their mission is the cultivation of ethical behaviour among cybersecurity practitioners. This Code of Ethics lays a robust foundation for cybersecurity professionals, ensuring that their actions and decisions uphold the highest standards of trust, responsibility, and ethical practice.

ISC2 members are professionals who must act ethically. They should make tough ethical choices and help each other do the right thing. While the board knows it should guide certificate holders on ethical decisions, it doesn't want to control or judge them. The board's job is to keep the certification honest. The ISC2 board recognizes its responsibility to maintain the integrity of the certification. It accepts that, from time to time, the good of the profession may require it to disassociate the profession from egregious behaviour on the part of a particular certificate holder. It intends to deal with necessary complaints in a timely manner, for example, revoking the certificate, like CISSP, issued to a professional for not adhering to the ISC2 Code of Ethics.

The ISC2 Code of Ethics is based on four fundamental canons. These canons provide a high-level framework for ethical decision-making in the field of cybersecurity.

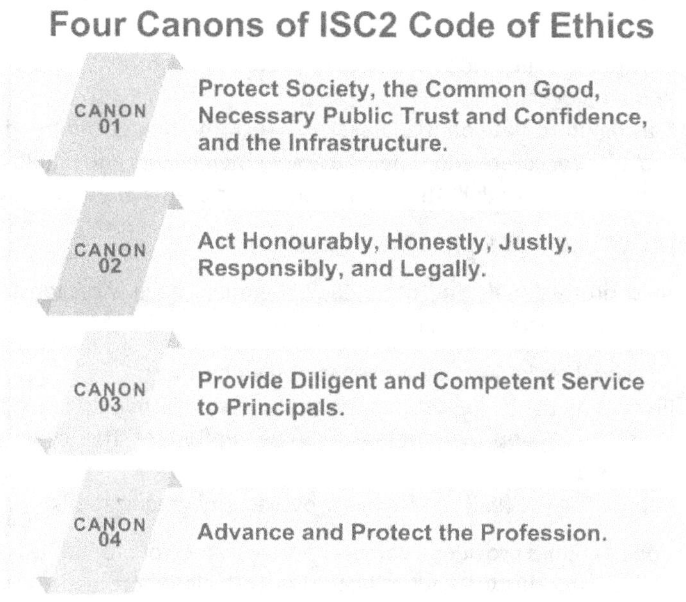

A) Canon 1: *Protect Society, the Common Good, Necessary Public Trust and Confidence, and the Infrastructure.*

ISC2-certified professionals and other ISC2 members have a responsibility to protect society, the common good, and the infrastructure from cyber-attacks. This includes:

- Promoting the security and resilience of organizations and individuals.
- Educating others about cybersecurity risks and how to mitigate them.
- Reporting vulnerabilities and security incidents to the appropriate authorities.
- Working to improve the cybersecurity posture of the profession and the industry as a whole.

B) Canon 2: *Act Honourably, Honestly, Justly, Responsibly, and Legally.*

ISC2-certified professionals and other ISC2 members are expected to act with integrity and professionalism in all aspects of their work. This includes:

- Being honest and truthful in their dealings with others.
- Treating others with respect and fairness.
- Complying with all applicable laws and regulations.
- Avoiding conflicts of interest.
- Acting in the best interests of their clients and employers.

C) Canon 3: *Provide Diligent and Competent Service to Principals.*

ISC2-certified professionals and other ISC2 members have a responsibility to provide diligent and competent service to their clients and employers. This includes:

- Using their skills and knowledge to protect the interests of their clients and employers.
- Staying up-to-date on the latest cybersecurity threats and trends.
- Providing accurate and timely advice to their clients and employers.
- Avoiding any conduct that could harm their clients or employers.

D) Canon 4: *Advance and Protect the Profession*

ISC2-certified professionals and other ISC2 members have a responsibility to advance and protect the cybersecurity profession. This includes:

- Sharing their knowledge and expertise with others.
- Promoting the highest standards of professionalism in the field.
- Working to improve the public's perception of the cybersecurity profession.
- Supporting the $(ISC)^2$ and other cybersecurity organizations.

The ISC2 Code of Ethics provides a comprehensive framework for ethical conduct in the field of cybersecurity. By adhering to these principles, professionals ensure that they are trusted guardians of digital information, upholding the highest standards of integrity, responsibility, and professionalism. As the digital landscape continues to evolve, the ISC2 Code of Ethics remains a vital guide, steering cybersecurity professionals towards ethical and effective practices.

1.10 Understand Governance Processes

In the ever-evolving landscape of cybersecurity, organizations need robust governance processes to navigate the complex challenges posed by cyber threats. For every organisation, data is a valuable commodity, and cyber threats are becoming more sophisticated. The need for effective governance processes in cybersecurity cannot be overstated. Governance serves as the foundation for managing risks, ensuring compliance, and fostering a proactive cybersecurity culture within an organization. Cybersecurity governance is driven by the following three principles.

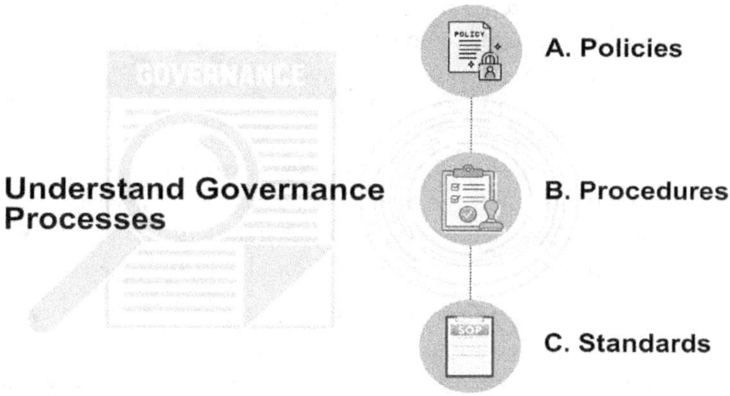

1.10.1 Policies

Cybersecurity policies are strategic directives that outline an organization's approach to safeguarding its information assets. They provide a high-level overview of the organization's stance on security, setting the tone for the entire cybersecurity framework. Policies are high-level statements that define the organization's approach to cybersecurity. They are typically approved by the board of directors or senior management and communicate the organization's expectations for all employees.

A) Organizational Policies:

1. **Clear and concise:** Policies should be easy to understand and follow, even for employees with no technical expertise. In most organizations, policies are published on their intranet sites for employees to access quickly. New joiners are required to go through the policies to understand them before starting their work. Few organizations mandate their employees revisit important (e.g., ISMS) policies and update their understanding periodically.
2. **Comprehensive:** Policies should cover all aspects of cybersecurity, from information security to incident response.
3. **Aligned with business objectives:** Policies should be designed to protect the organization's most valuable assets and support its business goals.

4. **Reviewed and updated regularly:** Policies should be reviewed and updated regularly to ensure that they are practical and up-to-date.

B) Examples of Cybersecurity Policies:

1. **Information security policy:** This policy defines the organization's requirements for protecting the confidentiality, integrity, and availability of its information assets.
2. **Acceptable use policy: This** policy defines the acceptable uses of the organization's information and technology resources.
3. **Incident response policy:** This policy outlines the steps that the organization will take to respond to and recover from a cybersecurity incident.
4. **Access Control Policies:** Define rules and principles governing access to information systems and data. This policy guides how the organisations assets can be accessed by employees, vendors, suppliers, and customers and their limitations.
5. **Data Protection Policies:** Specify how sensitive data should be handled, stored, and transmitted. The policies are designed to meet the regulatory obligations in the geographical location where the data is being generated, accessed, modified, processed, parsed, stored, and destroyed.

Creating effective policies involves collaboration between cybersecurity experts, legal teams, and key stakeholders. It is essential to ensure that policies are clear, concise, and aligned with the organization's overall objectives. Once developed, policies must be communicated widely, and employees should receive training to understand and adhere to them.

1.10.2 Procedures

Procedures are detailed step-by-step instructions that operationalize the principles outlined in policies. They provide a roadmap for implementing security measures and responding to various scenarios. They are typically developed by the organization's IT department and are used to implement the organization's cybersecurity policies. The main goal of developing procedures is to translate an organisation's Policies into a plan of Action that can be implemented by various teams responsible for enforcing the specific policy.

A) Qualities of Procedures:

1. **Specific and step-by-step:** Procedures should be detailed enough so that employees can follow them without any difficulty. They should also be documented sequentially and easily understood.
2. **Easy to understand:** Procedures should be written in plain language and should avoid using technical jargon and acronyms to avoid confusion and misunderstanding. Many organisations create procedure documents in regional languages to ensure the end user is able to understand it in his language. Pictures and diagrams can also be added for ease of

understanding of the procedures. The use of specific colours is also encouraged to highlight specific instructions. E.g. Red colour is used to highlight danger; Yellow is used for caution. This clarity and currency of procedures ensure that everyone is well-informed and prepared for any cybersecurity situation.

3. **Up-to-date:** Procedures should be reviewed and updated regularly, as necessary, to reflect changes in the organization's environment and technology. Your active involvement in this process is crucial, as it ensures that the procedures are always relevant and effective.

B) Examples of Cybersecurity Procedures:

1. **Access request Procedure:** Explain how users can request access to systems and data. This ensures that only authorized personnel can access and modify sensitive information, enhancing overall security.
2. **Incident Response Plan:** This plan explains the established approach for responding to and managing cybersecurity incidents, minimizing damage and recovery time.
3. **Patch Management Procedure:** This procedure explains how and when security patches should be deployed to software and systems, addressing vulnerabilities and preventing exploitation by malicious actors.
4. **Multi-Factor Authentication (MFA) procedure:** This procedure explains how to implement MFA, which adds a layer of security by requiring users to provide multiple forms of identification for access, reducing the risk of unauthorized entry.
5. **Data Backup and Recovery Procedure:** This procedure explains the steps to regularly back up critical data and establish a robust recovery plan to minimize data loss and downtime in the event of a cyber-incident.

1.10.3 Standards

Standards are technical specifications that define how information systems should be implemented and configured. In cybersecurity, standards set the benchmarks for technical controls, processes, and protocols. They are often industry-recognized and provide a common language for evaluating and comparing cybersecurity measures. These standards are typically developed by industry organizations or government agencies and are used to ensure that information systems are secure.

Various cyber security standards exist globally. Adhering to established standards helps organizations achieve compliance, avoid legal repercussions, and ensure customer trust. International Organizations spread over vast geographical areas may be subjected to different regulations at various locations. Several cybersecurity standards are widely recognized and adopted globally to guide organizations in implementing effective cybersecurity practices.

A) Examples of Standards:

1. **ISO/IEC 27001:** An international standard for Information Security Management Systems (ISMS), providing a framework for establishing, implementing, maintaining, and continually improving information security.
2. **NIST Cybersecurity Framework (CSF):** Developed by the National Institute of Standards and Technology (NIST), this framework offers guidelines and best practices for improving cybersecurity risk management.
3. **PCI DSS (Payment Card Industry Data Security Standard):** A set of security standards designed to ensure that all companies that accept, process, store, or transmit credit card information maintain a secure environment.
4. **SOC 2 (Service Organization Control 2):** Developed by the American Institute of CPAs (AICPA), SOC 2 sets criteria for managing customer data based on five "trust service criteria" – security, availability, processing integrity, confidentiality, and privacy.
5. **COBIT (Control Objectives for Information and Related Technologies):** A framework developed by ISACA that provides a comprehensive governance and management approach for enterprise information and technology.
6. **CMMC (Cybersecurity Maturity Model Certification):** Developed by the U.S. Department of Defense (DoD), CMMC is a framework that assesses and enhances the cybersecurity posture of defense contractors.
7. **ITIL (Information Technology Infrastructure Library):** A set of practices for IT service management (ITSM) that focuses on aligning IT services with the needs of the business.

   The above are only examples of standards that will evolve over time or a new standards will be established. Therefore, you don't need to memorize them, but rather understand the core components and the reasons they were developed.

1.10.4 Cybersecurity Regulations and Laws

Cybercrime is a global problem that is constantly evolving. Cybercriminals are developing new and sophisticated methods of attack and targeting a wide range of victims, from individuals to large corporations. Cybersecurity regulations and laws are important because they help to protect individuals, organizations, and governments from cybercrime. They also help to promote trust in the digital economy. Cybersecurity regulations and laws help to deter cybercrime by imposing penalties on those who commit cybercrimes. They also help to raise awareness of cybersecurity risks and promote best practices.

A) Benefits of cybersecurity regulations and laws:

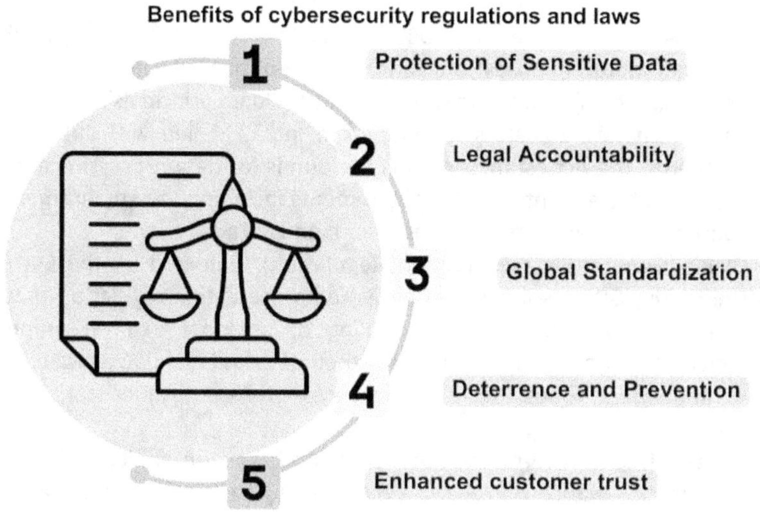

1. **Protection of Sensitive Data:** Cybersecurity regulations and laws establish the standards and obligations for protecting sensitive information. In a world where data breaches are on the rise, these regulations serve as a crucial shield, compelling organizations to implement robust security measures to safeguard the privacy and integrity of personal and corporate data.
2. **Legal Accountability:** Regulations create a legal framework that holds organizations accountable for the security of their digital assets. In the absence of comprehensive laws, the repercussions of a cyber incident might be ambiguous. Regulations provide clarity on liabilities, ensuring that negligent entities face legal consequences for failing to protect against cyber threats adequately.
3. **Global Standardization:** As the digital landscape transcends geographical boundaries, a patchwork of regional and international regulations helps create a common ground. Global standards, such as the GDPR (General Data Protection Regulation), facilitate international collaboration and ensure that organizations operating across borders adhere to consistent cybersecurity practices.
4. **Deterrence and Prevention:** The existence of cybersecurity laws deters malicious actors. Knowing the legal consequences of cybercrimes discourages potential attackers, contributing to the prevention of cyber incidents. Regulations, therefore, play a vital role in shaping the risk landscape and promoting a cybersecurity culture.
5. **Enhanced customer trust:** Cybersecurity regulations and laws can help organizations to build trust with their customers by demonstrating that they are taking steps to protect their data. This can lead to increased customer loyalty and business opportunities.

B) Key Cybersecurity Regulations and Laws:

1. **DPDP Act:** Digital Personal Data Protection Act, 2023 applies to digital personal data, imposes obligations on entities that qualify as 'data fiduciaries', establishes data subject rights for 'data principals', and generally allows outward transfers of data from India. In line with international standards, the Act establishes lawful grounds for data processing and data subject rights and introduces requirements including the appointment of a consent manager, vendor management, and data security.
2. **GDPR (General Data Protection Regulation):** Enforced by the European Union, the GDPR is a comprehensive data protection regulation that sets stringent standards for the handling of personal data. It empowers individuals with greater control over their data and mandates organizations to implement robust security measures. Non-compliance can result in severe fines.
3. **HIPAA (Health Insurance Portability and Accountability Act):** In the healthcare sector, HIPAA is a critical regulation that mandates the protection of sensitive patient information. Covered entities, such as healthcare providers and insurers, must adhere to strict security standards to ensure the confidentiality and integrity of health information.
4. **CCPA (California Consumer Privacy Act):** Operating in one of the most technologically advanced states, the CCPA sets a precedent for data protection in the United States. It grants California residents greater control over their personal information and requires businesses to disclose their data practices. Non-compliance can lead to penalties and legal action.
5. **Computer Fraud and Abuse Act (CFAA):** The CFAA is a foundational law in the United States that addresses computer-related crimes. It criminalizes unauthorized access to computer systems and provides a legal framework to prosecute hackers and individuals engaging in cybercrimes.

These are just a few examples of essential cybersecurity regulations and laws. There are many other regulations and laws in place around the world, Cyber Security regulations and laws play a pivotal role in establishing a secure and accountable environment. They provide the legal scaffolding necessary for organizations to navigate the complexities of cyberspace, safeguard sensitive information, and deter malicious actors. Organizations should be aware of the cybersecurity regulations and laws that apply to them and should take steps to comply with those regulations and laws. This will help them to reduce their risk of cybercrime and improve their overall cybersecurity posture.

These examples highlight just a fraction of vital cybersecurity laws, which are crucial for creating a safer, more accountable digital world. Staying compliant isn't just legal—it's essential for protecting what matters most and building trust in an ever-evolving threat landscape.

Domain 2: Business Continuity (BC), Disaster Recovery (DR) & Incident Response Concepts

In the increasingly interconnected world of digital business, the ability to withstand and recover from unexpected disruptions is essential. Organizations might face a variety of threats that could disrupt their operations or compromise their data, such as Cyberattacks, natural disasters, and unforeseen incidents. Under such circumstances, Business continuity (BC), Disaster recovery (DR), and Incident response (IR) plans are essential for any organization that wants to protect itself from disruptive events. By having these plans in place, organizations can reduce the impact of disruptive events and minimize the disruption to their business operations. Let us look at these plans closely.

2.1 Understanding Business Continuity (BC)

In the dynamic and interconnected world of cybersecurity, understanding the principles of Business Continuity (BC) is crucial. Business Continuity refers to an organization's ability to maintain essential functions and recover rapidly in the event of a disruption, be it a cyber incident, natural disaster, or any unforeseen crisis. The purpose of business continuity (BC) is to ensure that an organization can continue to operate in the event of a disruption, without affecting its customers. This disruption could be due to a variety of factors, such as a natural disaster, a cyberattack, or a human error.

2.1.1 Purpose

Organizations of all sizes are vulnerable to disruptions. Disruptions could happen due to several reasons, such as natural disaster like earthquake, flood, fire, etc. This can have a significant impact on an organization's bottom line, reputation, and customer trust. In addition, many organizations are required to have Business Continuity plans in place in order to comply with relevant regulations. For example, the General Data Protection Regulation (GDPR) requires organizations to have a plan in place to protect the personal data of European citizens in the event of a data breach.

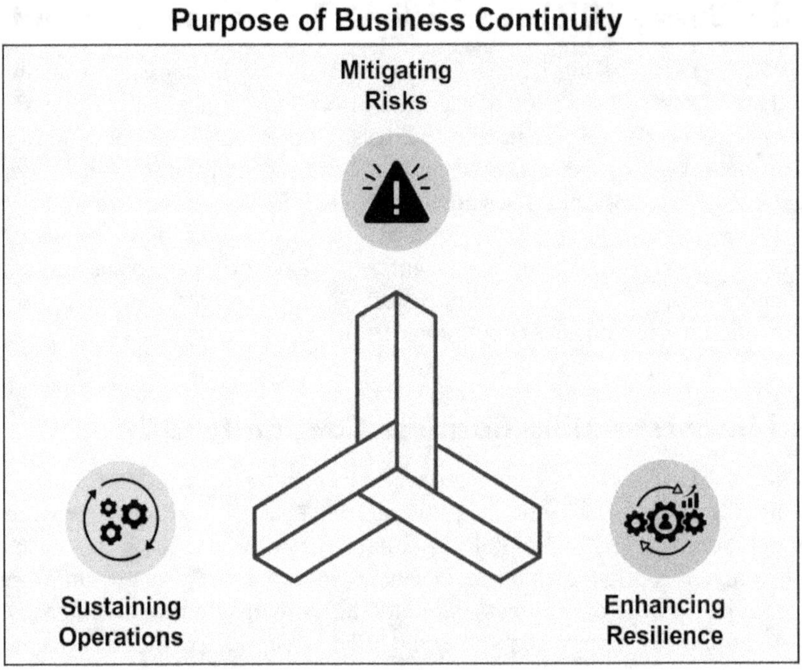

A) **Sustaining Operations:** Business Continuity ensures that core business functions continue seamlessly, even in the face of disruptions. This involves identifying critical processes, resources, and dependencies to establish a roadmap for sustained operations.

B) **Mitigating Risks:** By comprehensively assessing potential risks and vulnerabilities, Business Continuity plan allows organizations to implement measures to mitigate these risks proactively. This includes cybersecurity threats, which can disrupt operations and compromise sensitive data.

C) **Enhancing Resilience:** The overarching purpose of Business Continuity is to make an organization resilient. Resilience ensures not just recovering from disruptions but adapting and evolving in the aftermath, learning from experiences to improve future response capabilities.

2.1.2 Importance

Business Continuity planning is important because disruptions usually happen abruptly without any notice. An organisation prepared to handle such disruptions can achieve the following goals.

Importance of Business Continuity

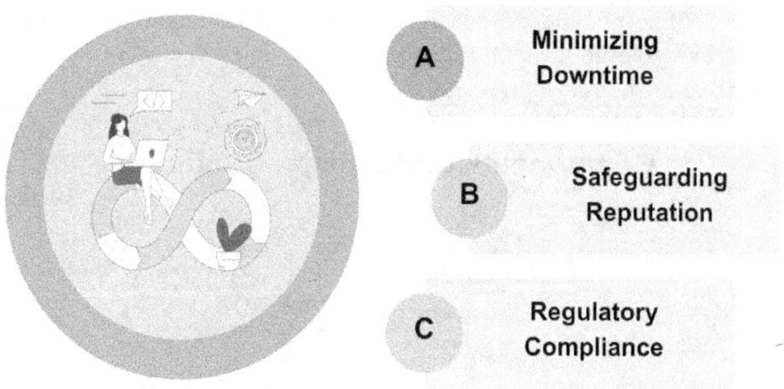

A) **Minimizing Downtime:** A downtime can translate into significant financial losses and damage to reputation. Business Continuity strategies minimize downtime by enabling quick recovery and maintaining critical operations, ensuring that the organization remains operational during and after a disruptive incident.

B) **Safeguarding Reputation:** A well-executed Business Continuity plan helps maintain customer trust by demonstrating a commitment to operational resilience and security. In the event of a cyber incident, an organization's ability to recover quickly and transparently can mitigate reputational damage.

C) **Regulatory Compliance:** Many industries have regulatory requirements that mandate the implementation of Business Continuity plans. Adhering to these regulations not only ensures legal compliance but also aligns with best practices for cybersecurity risk management.

2.1.3 Components

Business Continuity comprises several interconnected components, each playing an important role in ensuring a comprehensive and effective strategy. These components are as below:

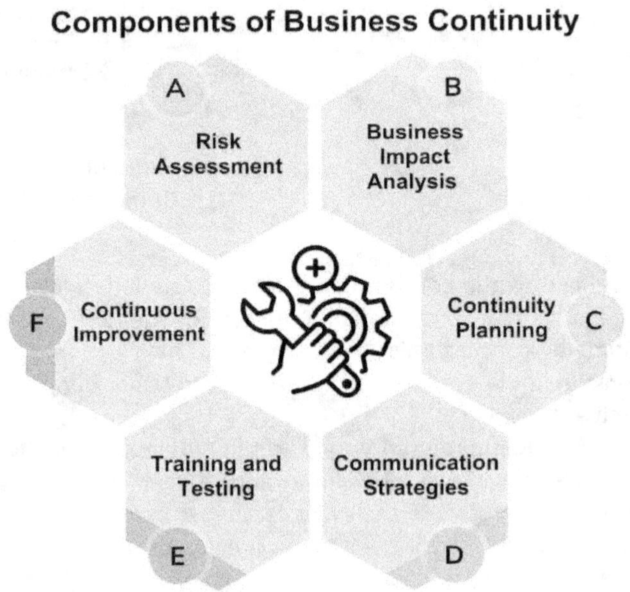

A) **Risk Assessment:** Understanding and assessing risks is the foundation of Business Continuity. This involves identifying potential threats, evaluating vulnerabilities, and quantifying the impact of disruptions. Cybersecurity risks, including data breaches and system compromises, are integral considerations in this assessment.

B) **Business Impact Analysis (BIA):** BIA involves analyzing the potential impact of disruptions on critical business functions. It helps prioritize resources and efforts by identifying the most essential processes and systems. In the context of cybersecurity, BIA assesses the impact of data breaches, loss of sensitive information, and disruptions to IT infrastructure.

C) **Continuity Planning:** Developing a detailed continuity plan is a cornerstone of Business Continuity. This plan outlines specific actions, responsibilities, and processes to be followed during and after a disruption. Regarding cybersecurity, the plan includes incident response procedures, data recovery processes, and communication strategies.

D) **Communication Strategies:** Effective communication is vital during a crisis. Business Continuity includes strategies for internal and external communication to keep stakeholders informed and mitigate confusion. This is particularly critical in cybersecurity incidents, where timely and accurate information can prevent further damage.

E) **Training and Testing:** Regular training and testing ensure that employees are familiar with Business Continuity procedures and can execute them efficiently. This includes simulated exercises to evaluate the effectiveness of the Business Continuity plan, especially in scenarios involving cyber threats.

F) **Continuous Improvement:** Business Continuity is a dynamic process that requires constant evaluation and improvement. Regular reviews, updates, and adjustments based on lessons learned from incidents or exercises contribute to the adaptability and effectiveness of the Business Continuity strategy in the face of evolving cybersecurity threats.

2.2 Understanding Disaster Recovery (DR)

Disaster recovery is an organization's method of regaining access and functionality to its IT infrastructure after events like a natural disaster, cyber-attack, or even business disruptions following a natural or human-induced disaster. A variety of disaster recovery (DR) methods can be part of a disaster recovery plan. DR is one aspect of business continuity.

2.2.1 Purpose

Disaster Recovery (DR) refers to the systematic approach an organization takes to respond to and recover from disruptive events. The purpose of DR is to restore an organization's operations to normal after a disaster. A disaster can be any event that disrupts the organization's ability to operate, such as a fire, flood, cyber-attack, or natural disaster.

A) **Minimizing Downtime:** At its core, the purpose of Disaster Recovery plan is to minimize downtime in the aftermath of a disaster. Whether the disaster is a cyber incident, a natural calamity, or any unforeseen event, Disaster Recovery strategies aim to ensure that critical systems and operations can be restored promptly.

B) **Protecting Data Integrity:** In cybersecurity, Disaster Recovery plays a crucial role in protecting data integrity. This involves creating backups, implementing secure storage solutions, and establishing protocols for data recovery in the event of a cyber-attack or data breach.

C) **Ensuring Business Continuity:** Disaster Recovery is integral to maintaining business continuity. By having robust recovery mechanisms in place, organizations can continue essential operations and services even when faced with significant disruptions, safeguarding their overall continuity.

2.2.2 Importance

A Disaster Recovery plan is essential because all organizations are vulnerable to disasters. Disasters often occur unannounced and can significantly impact an organization's bottom line, reputation, and customer trust. In addition, many organizations are required to have DR plans in place to comply with relevant regulations. For example, the HIPAA Security Rule requires healthcare organizations to have a DR plan in place to protect the health information of their patients in the event of a disaster.

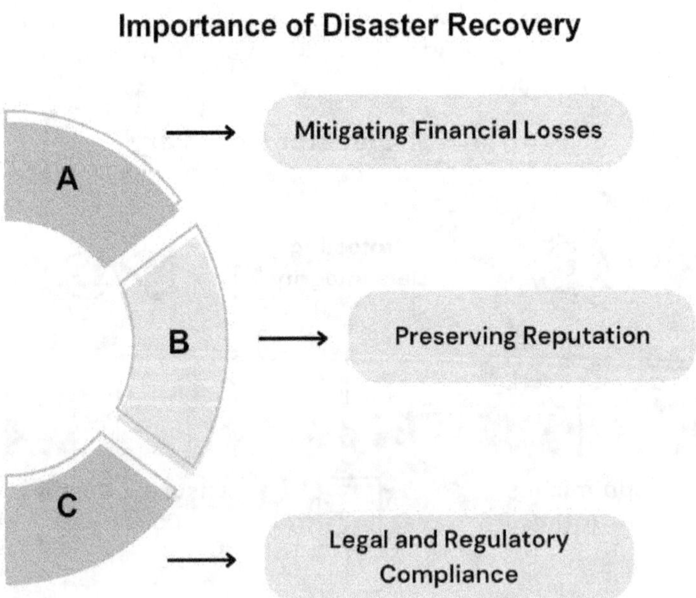

A) **Mitigating Financial Losses:** Downtime resulting from a disaster, especially a cyber incident, can result in substantial financial losses. Disaster Recovery minimizes these losses by enabling a swift recovery, reducing the impact on revenue streams, and preventing potential long-term financial repercussions.

B) **Preserving Reputation:** A prompt and effective recovery from a disaster, particularly a cyber-attack, is crucial for preserving an organization's reputation. Stakeholders, including customers and partners, expect an organization to bounce back resiliently from incidents and maintain the trust they place in its services.

C) **Legal and Regulatory Compliance:** Adherence to legal and regulatory requirements is crucial in the cybersecurity landscape. Many regulations, like HIPPA, mandate the implementation of Disaster Recovery plans to safeguard data and ensure the continuity of operations. Failure to comply with these requirements can lead to legal consequences and damage an organization's standing.

2.2.3 Components

A Disaster Recovery plan typically consists of the following components.

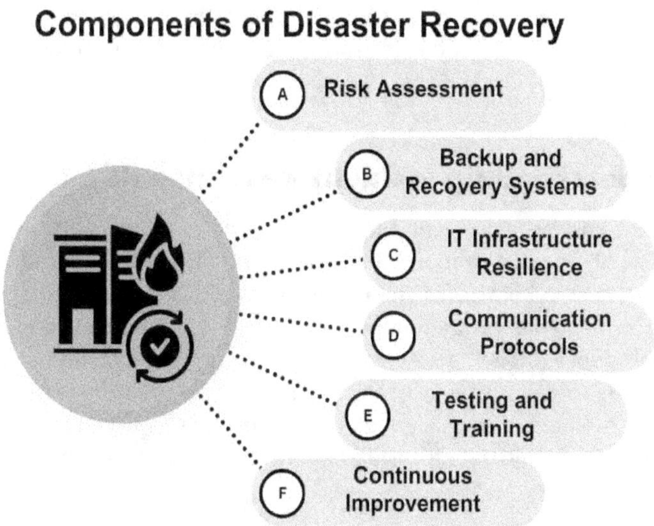

A) **Risk Assessment:** Similar to Business Continuity, Disaster Recovery starts with a thorough risk assessment. This involves identifying potential threats and vulnerabilities that could lead to disasters, including cyber threats such as malware, ransomware, and denial-of-service attacks.

B) **Backup and Recovery Systems:** A robust Disaster Recovery plan includes well-defined backup and recovery systems. These systems involve regular and secure backups of critical data and systems. Backups are crucial for restoring systems to a pre-incident state and mitigating data loss resulting from cyber-attacks.

C) **IT Infrastructure Resilience:** Ensuring the resilience of the IT infrastructure is a fundamental component of Disaster Recovery. This includes redundant systems, failover mechanisms, and the capability to switch to alternative resources rapidly.

D) **Communication Protocols:** Effective communication is vital during a disaster. Clear communication protocols ensure that relevant stakeholders are informed promptly, both internally and externally. In the case of cybersecurity incidents, communication becomes even more critical to managing the public relations aspect and keeping stakeholders informed of the situation.

E) **Testing and Training:** Regular testing of Disaster Recovery plans through simulated exercises helps identify weaknesses and ensures that the recovery processes are effective. Training employees to respond appropriately during a disaster, including cyber incidents, enhances the organization's overall readiness.

F) **Continuous Improvement:** Disaster Recovery is an evolving process that requires continuous improvement. Regular reviews, updates, and adjustments based on lessons learned from incidents or exercises contribute to the adaptability and effectiveness of the Disaster Recovery strategies.

2.3 Understanding Incident Response (IR)

An incident can be any event that disrupts the confidentiality, integrity, or availability of an organization's information or systems. Common types of incidents include cyberattacks, data breaches, and system failures. In a dynamic and interconnected organization, minor and major incidents occur periodically. Incident response (IR) is the process by which an organization detects, analyses, and responds to various types of incidents. The goal of Incident response is to minimize the impact of an incident on the organization's business operations and to restore systems and data to regular operation as quickly as possible.

2.3.1 Purpose

At its core, incident response serves as the structured approach to handling and managing the aftermath of a security incident. The primary purpose is to minimize damage and reduce recovery time and costs. When a security incident occurs, whether it's a data breach, malware infection, or a sophisticated cyber-attack, an effective incident response plan ensures that the organization can swiftly identify, contain, eradicate, and recover from the incident. At its core, incident response is not merely reactive process; it is also a proactive strategy to strengthen an organization's overall cybersecurity posture. By learning from each incident, organizations can continuously improve their security measures, identify vulnerabilities, and enhance their ability to prevent future incidents.

Purpose of Incident Response

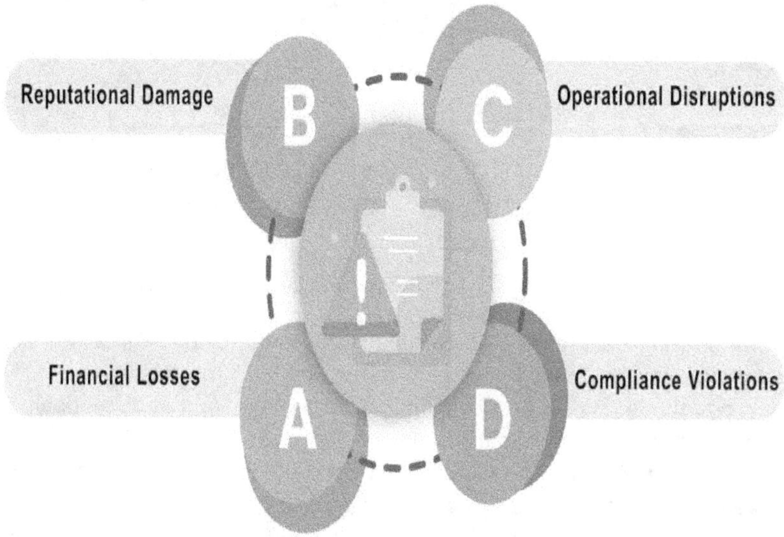

By responding quickly and effectively to incidents, organizations can reduce the following:

A) **Financial Losses:** Incidents can lead to significant financial losses through lost revenue, damage to reputation, and fines and penalties.
B) **Reputational Damage:** Incidents can damage an organization's reputation and erode customer trust.
C) **Operational Disruptions:** Incidents can disrupt an organization's operations and lead to productivity losses.
D) **Compliance Violations:** Incidents can violate industry regulations and lead to legal penalties.

2.3.2 Importance

Incident response is an essential part of any organization's cybersecurity program. Organizations of all sizes are at risk of security incidents, and even the most well-defended organizations can be breached. By having a well-defined and tested incident response plan in place, organizations can be prepared to respond to incidents quickly and effectively, and minimize their impact. Several vital factors highlight its significance:

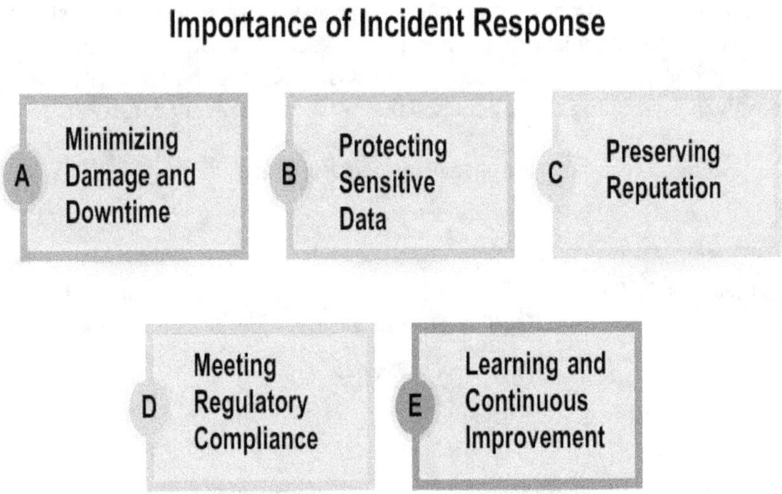

A) **Minimizing Damage and Downtime:** Swift and effective incident response minimizes the impact of a security incident. By containing the incident promptly, organizations can limit the damage and reduce downtime, ensuring business continuity.

B) **Protecting Sensitive Data:** In an era where data is often considered the most valuable asset, incident response plays a crucial role in protecting sensitive information. Timely identification and containment prevent unauthorized access and exfiltration of data.

C) **Preserving Reputation:** A security incident can have severe implications for an organization's reputation. A well-executed incident response plan can demonstrate transparency, accountability, and a commitment to security, helping to maintain trust with customers, partners, and stakeholders.

D) **Meeting Regulatory Compliance:** Many industries are subject to stringent data protection regulations. Incident response is vital for meeting compliance requirements by demonstrating that the organization has taken appropriate measures to safeguard information and respond to incidents.

E) **Learning and Continuous Improvement:** Every incident provides valuable insights. By thoroughly analyzing incidents, organizations can identify weaknesses in their security infrastructure, update policies and procedures, and continuously improve their overall cybersecurity posture.

2.3.3 Components

An effective incident response plan is a comprehensive framework comprised of several interconnected components:

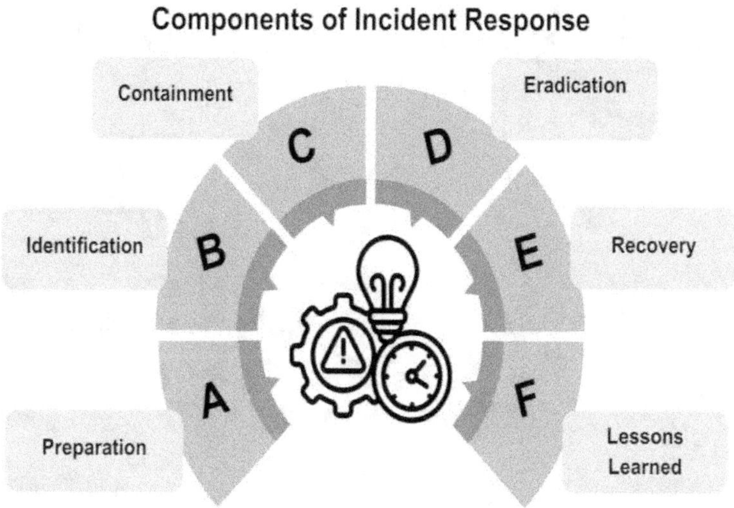

A) **Preparation:** This involves establishing an incident response team, defining roles and responsibilities, and developing an incident response plan that is tailored to the organization's specific needs. Training and regular drills ensure that the team is well-prepared for an actual incident.
B) **Identification:** The identification phase involves recognizing and confirming the occurrence of a security incident. This includes monitoring for unusual activities, analyzing logs, and leveraging intrusion detection systems to identify potential threats swiftly.
C) **Containment:** Once an incident is identified, the next step is to contain it to prevent further damage. This may involve isolating affected systems, blocking malicious activity, and taking other measures to limit the incident's impact.
D) **Eradication:** After containment, the focus shifts to eradicating the root cause of the incident. This may involve removing malware, closing vulnerabilities, and implementing patches to ensure that the same incident does not recur.
E) **Recovery:** The recovery phase involves restoring systems and data to normal operations. This includes verifying system integrity, applying lessons learned from the incident to improve security, and ensuring that all systems are fully functional.
F) **Lessons Learned:** A critical component of incident response is the post-incident analysis. This phase involves a thorough review of the incident, identifying what worked well and what could be improved. These lessons learned inform updates to the incident response plan and contribute to ongoing security enhancements.

Incident response is an essential part of any organisation's cybersecurity program. By having a well-defined and tested incident response plan in place, organisations can be prepared to respond to incidents quickly and effectively and minimise their impact.

Domain 3: Access Control Concepts

Access Control (AC) is a fundamental concept essential for protecting sensitive information, systems, and networks. It ensures that users are who they claim to be and have appropriate permissions to access company resources and assets necessary for their roles. Essentially, access control involves selectively restricting access to data, tools, systems, networks, and other critical components. The access control policy defines the measures for both physical security—such as locked access to server rooms—and logical security, limiting software and network access to safeguard data. While traditional perimeter defenses like firewalls—such as packet filters, proxies, and stateful inspection devices—play a role, they are no longer sufficient on their own. Access control is the key component of a comprehensive defense-in-depth strategy, allowing organizations to adapt policies dynamically to emerging threats, isolate compromised systems, and minimize damage after breaches. Most security professionals recognize that robust access control is vital to their organization's security posture.

Access Control Types: Access control is divided into two main categories: Physical Access Control and Logical Access Control. In this domain, we will examine both controls closely and understand their importance in Cyber Security.

3.1 Understanding Physical Security Controls

They are an essential aspect of protecting people, property, and physical assets from potential damage or loss. While Logical Cybersecurity often takes the spotlight during discussions, physical security is equally significant. No matter how strong your logical access controls, like firewall, IPS, etc, are, they won't help if an attacker gains physical access to the organisation's digital assets, such as computers, network routers or storage devices. Physical security controls are primarily concerned with ensuring the physical safety of facilities, individuals, and assets by employing measures to deter, detect, and respond to physical, i.e. real-world threats. This is the initial layer of security for a campus, building, office, or other physical space designed to deter physical threats.

Physical barriers such as fences, walls, and vehicle barriers are the outermost layer of physical security. Tall fencing, topped with barbed wire, razor wire, or metal spikes, is often emplaced on the perimeter of a property, generally with some signage that warns people not to attempt to enter the area. Physical access control can be achieved by a human, such as a Security guard, bouncer, or receptionist. Mechanical means such as locks and keys become a problem with large user populations and any user turnover. Keys quickly become unmanageable, often forcing the adoption of electronic access control. Electronic access control helps to manage large user populations, controlling for user life cycle times, dates, and individual access points. These access control systems are often interfaced with turnstiles for entry control in buildings to prevent unauthorised access. The use of turnstiles also reduces the need for additional security personnel to monitor each individual entering the building, allowing faster throughput.

A) Categorizing Physical Security: Physical security can be categorized into various sections based on the target and the nature of threats. One standard categorization is based on controlling access to specific areas or assets. This involves preventing unauthorized individuals, whether external or internal, from accessing restricted areas. Examples include restricting public access to corporate headquarters, preventing on-site third parties from sensitive work areas, and securing mission-critical locations like server rooms.

B) Types of Physical Attacks: Physical attacks can take different forms, including breaking into secure data centers, infiltrating restricted areas of a building, or gaining unauthorized access to terminals. Attackers may attempt to steal or damage critical IT assets such as servers and storage media, gain access to terminals used for mission-critical applications, steal information via USB devices, or upload malware onto systems.

3.1.1 Physical Access Controls (PAC)

While digital access controls, such as authentication and authorization mechanisms, are commonly discussed, the physical aspect of access control is equally significant. Physical access controls form the first line of defense against unauthorized access to critical assets. Whether it is a data center, server room, or an organization's headquarters, controlling physical access is fundamental for ensuring the integrity and confidentiality of sensitive information.

Purpose of Physical Access Controls

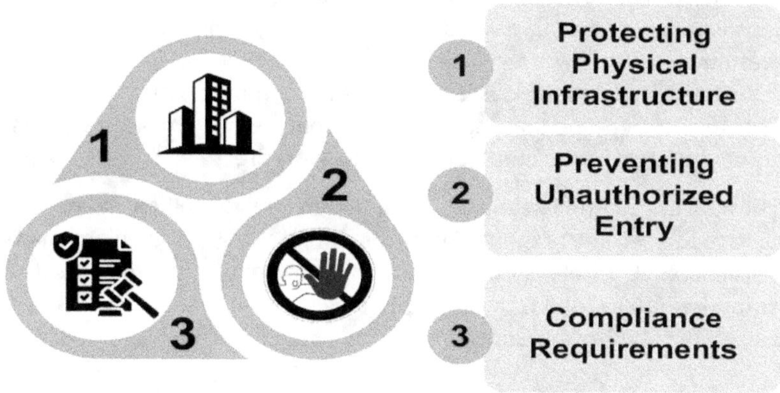

A) Purpose: The primary function of Physical Access Controls is to:

1. **Protecting Physical Infrastructure:** Critical hardware, servers, and networking equipment reside in physical spaces. Robust physical access controls prevent unauthorized individuals from tampering with or stealing these assets, safeguarding the infrastructure's integrity.
2. **Preventing Unauthorized Entry:** Unauthorized personnel gaining physical access to sensitive areas can lead to various security breaches. Physical access controls, such as access cards, biometric systems, and security personnel, prevent individuals without proper authorization from entering restricted zones.
3. **Compliance Requirements:** Various regulatory frameworks and compliance standards mandate stringent physical access control measures. Adhering to these requirements not only ensures legal compliance but also demonstrates a commitment to securing sensitive information.

B) Physical Access Controls Strategies: Deploying adequate physical access controls involves a strategic combination of technology, policies, and practices. Here are some key implementation strategies:

1. **Access Control Systems:** Utilize access control systems that integrate electronic locks, access cards, biometrics, and other technologies. These systems provide a centralized and programmable way to manage physical access.
2. **Biometric Authentication:** Implement biometric authentication methods, such as fingerprint or retina scans, to enhance the accuracy and security of physical access controls. Biometrics add an additional layer of identity verification.
3. **Surveillance and Monitoring:** Employ surveillance cameras and monitoring systems to track and record physical access. This not only acts as a deterrent but also aids in investigations in the event of a security incident.

4. **Physical Barriers:** Use physical barriers, such as gates, turnstiles, and secure doors, to control the flow of individuals within a facility. These barriers should be designed to withstand tampering and unauthorised entry attempts.
5. **Visitor Management Systems:** Implement robust visitor management systems to ensure that individuals without permanent access rights are appropriately vetted and supervised while on-site.

Physical access control is not just a part, but an integral and crucial part of any organization's security program. By implementing a well-designed and managed Physical Access Control system, organizations can help protect their assets from unauthorised access and reduce the risk of security incidents, emphasizing the gravity of the security measures.

3.1.2 Monitoring

Monitoring is a vital component of any physical access control system. By overseeing access points and other sensitive areas, organizations can detect and respond to unauthorized access attempts promptly. Surveillance involves deploying various mechanisms to observe and record activities within a facility, including security guards on patrol, burglar alarms, closed-circuit television (CCTV) systems, sound and movement sensors, activity logging, and additional physical monitoring devices like biometric scanners. In high-risk locations, more advanced detectors such as proximity, infrared, image, optical, temperature, smoke, and pressure sensors may be used to maintain a comprehensive view of the premises. Surveillance cameras, including CCTV cameras, are strategically positioned to assist in incident assessment and historical analysis.

Video monitoring alone does not guarantee a human response; a trained individual must monitor in real time to respond effectively, otherwise, video serves primarily as evidence collection for later review.

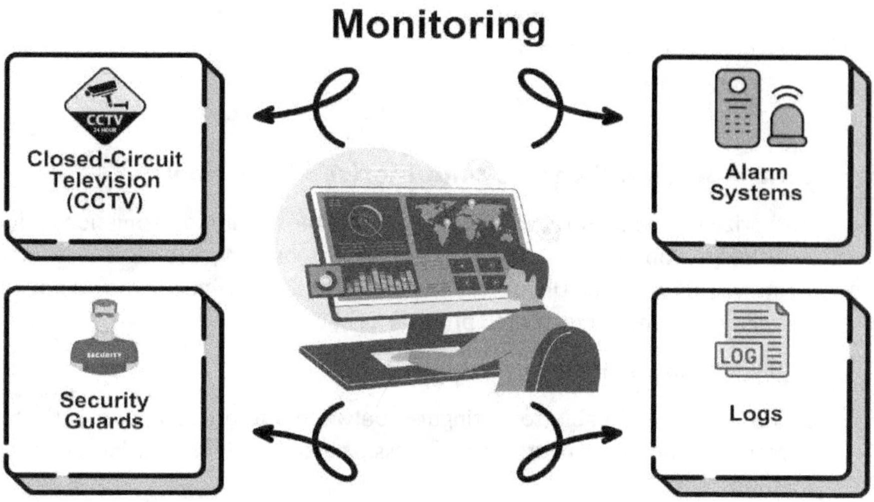

A) Monitoring Technologies: There are a variety of monitoring technologies that can be used to protect physical locations, including:

1. **Security Guards:** Security guards can monitor access control points and other sensitive areas, deter unauthorized access, and respond to security incidents.
2. **Closed-Circuit Television (CCTV):** CCTV cameras can monitor access control points and other sensitive areas. The footage can also be used to investigate security incidents and identify suspects.
3. **Alarm Systems:** Alarm systems can detect unauthorized access attempts and alert security personnel. They can be installed on doors, windows, and other vulnerable areas.
4. **Logs:** Access control systems typically generate logs of all access events. These logs can be reviewed to identify suspicious activity and to investigate security incidents.

B) Alarm Systems: Alarm systems play a pivotal role in notifying security personnel about potential breaches. These systems are designed to trigger alerts when specific conditions, such as unauthorized access or tampering, are detected. Alarms serve as an immediate response mechanism, initiating actions to address security incidents promptly.

Key Features of Alarm Systems:

1. **Intrusion Detection:** Alarm systems are equipped to detect unauthorized access attempts or breaches, triggering alarms for immediate attention.
2. **Tamper Detection:** Some systems include sensors that detect tampering with doors, windows, or other physical barriers, activating alarms as a preventive measure.

3. **Integration with Response Protocols:** Alarm systems are often integrated with response protocols, ensuring a rapid and coordinated reaction to security incidents.

3.1.3 Authorized versus Unauthorized Personnel

Authorized personnel are individuals who have been granted permission to enter a designated physical location, such as an office building, premises, production floor, warehouses, etc. Unauthorized personnel are individuals who do not have permission to enter a restricted physical location.

A) Distinguish Methods:

It is essential to be able to distinguish between authorized and unauthorized personnel to prevent unauthorized access. This can be done by using a variety of methods, such as:

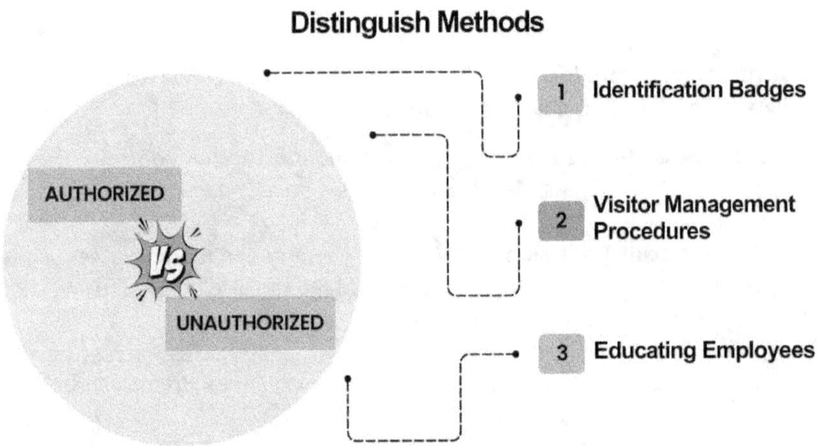

1. **Identification badges:** Identification badges can be used to identify authorized personnel visually. Most organizations issue Identification badges to their employees, vendors, suppliers, contractors, etc. The identification badge ought to be displayed at all times a person is present at the designated location. These identification badges are supposed to be worn around the neck. Usually, the employees have a specific colour badge, whereas visitors have different colour badges. The employees are allowed to keep the badge with them till the organisation employs them. In contrast, the visitors are required to return the badges while leaving the organisation premises.
2. **Visitor Management procedures:** Visitor management procedures can help ensure that visitors are correctly identified and authorized before entering a facility. Visitors are given unique identification badges that are different from those of employees. An employee mostly escorts visitors to various

parts of the organisation. Visitors are also given temporary and limited access to office equipment and Wi-Fi, which has the fewest privileges.

3. **Educating employees:** Employees should be educated on security best practices, such as not giving out their identification badges or not allowing unauthorized individuals to enter restricted areas.

B) Challenges in Managing Authorized and Unauthorized Access:

While the goal is to maintain a clear distinction between authorized and unauthorized personnel, several challenges exist:

1. **Social Engineering Attacks:** Manipulation of individuals to gain unauthorized access is a persistent challenge. Awareness programs are essential to mitigate the risk of social engineering attacks.
2. **Insider Threats:** Trusted individuals within an organization may pose a threat. Implementing role-based access controls and continuous monitoring helps detect and prevent insider threats.
3. **Credential Theft:** Unauthorized individuals may attempt to steal or replicate access credentials. Strong authentication mechanisms and encryption protocols are vital to prevent credential theft.

3.2 Understanding Logical Access Controls

Logical access control (LAC) is a set of security measures designed to regulate who and what can access computer systems and networks. These systems can be used to protect a wide range of assets, including data, applications, and systems. Logical access controls pertain to the digital mechanisms and policies that govern access to computer systems, networks, and data. Unlike physical access controls, which restrict entry to physical spaces, logical access controls focus on regulating virtual access points. Logical Access Control systems can also be integrated with other security systems, such as intrusion detection systems and security information and event management (SIEM) systems. Logical Access Control systems can help to prevent unauthorized access to computer systems and networks. This can help to reduce the risk of data breaches, malware infections, and other security incidents. This systems can help to streamline operations and improve efficiency. For example, LAC systems can be used to automate the user account provisioning process. Many industries have regulations that require organizations to implement Logical Access Control systems. For example, organizations that handle sensitive customer data are often required to implement Logical Access control systems to protect that data from unauthorized access.

3.2.1 Logical Access Controls (LAC)

The second category of Access control is Logical Access Control (LAC). It is further divided into Administrative Access Controls and Technical Access Control. We will examine both and understand their importance.

Types of Logical Access Controls

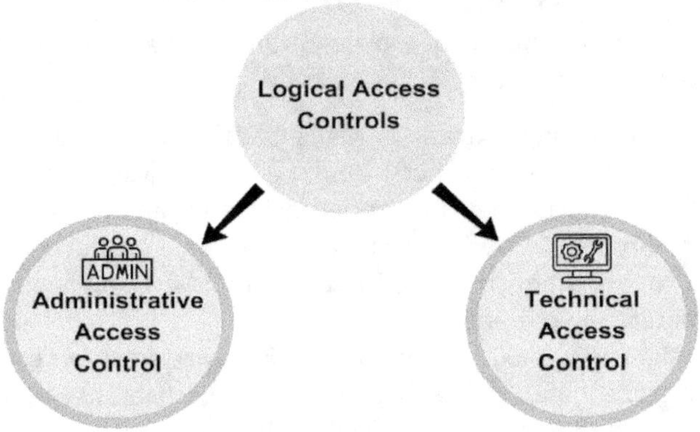

A) Administrative Access Control: Administrative access control includes organisation policies and procedures that outline various activities employees, visitors, contractors, and suppliers can and cannot perform. These policies are a set of rules and guidelines that define how administrative access to systems and data should be granted, managed, and revoked. These policies should be based on the organisation's risk assessment and should be tailored to the specific needs of the organisation. Administrative access controls are an essential part of any cybersecurity program. By implementing adequate administrative access controls, organisations can reduce the risk of unauthorised access to systems and data, which can help to prevent data breaches, security incidents, and compliance violations.

Below are a few examples of the most common policies adopted by organisations.

1. **Access Control Policy:** This policy outlines how access rights to systems are granted, reviewed, and revoked. It often includes user access, administrator access, and system-to-system access protocols.
2. **Acceptable Use Policy (AUP):** This policy details what employees are allowed and not allowed to do with organisational IT systems and services. Some organisations do not allow employees to use social media platforms, such as Facebook, YouTube, Spotify, etc., on office desktops or laptops.
3. **Mobile Device Policy:** This policy covers the security controls over devices like smartphones, tablets, and laptops, including those that fall under "Bring Your Own Device" (BYOD) programs.
4. **Password Policy:** Dictates requirements for password complexity, expiration, and reuse, aiming to ensure strong authentication.

5. **User Awareness and Training Policy:** This policy underlines the organisation's commitment to continuous security training and awareness programs for its employees.

Similarly, organisations have several procedures documented to perform specific tasks. A few examples are given below.

1. **Identity Handling Procedures:** Explains how user accounts should be created, maintained, changed, audited, suspended and disabled.
2. **Data handling procedures:** explains how to handle data, including collection, storage, processing, usage, and disposal.
3. **Incident response procedures:** Explains what steps the organisation will follow in the event of a data breach or other security incident.
4. **Data Retention and Destruction:** Explains how data retention periods and procedures, including secure methods for data disposal and destruction.
5. **Change Procedure:** Includes the procedure of logging a change request, getting approvals from the Change Advisory Board, rollback and verification procedure, etc.

Policies provide the strategic framework, expressing the organization's directives on access control, while procedures translate these directives into concrete actions. Together, they form the bedrock of a secure and resilient information system.

B) Technical Access Control: Technical access controls are security measures used to restrict access to computer systems, networks, and data. They are implemented through a combination of hardware and software solutions, each playing a pivotal role in creating a secure computing environment. Technical access controls are an important part of any cybersecurity program. By implementing effective technical access controls, organisations can reduce the risk of data breaches, improve compliance, reduce the risk of security incidents, and improve their overall security posture.

Hardware access controls are physical devices that are used to restrict access to systems and data. Common examples of hardware access controls include:

1. **Smart Cards:** Smart cards are plastic cards that contain a computer chip that stores the user's identity and authentication credentials. Smart cards are typically used in conjunction with an intelligent card reader to authenticate users to systems.
2. **Biometric Scanners:** Biometric scanners use physical characteristics, such as fingerprints, facial features, or iris scans, to authenticate users to systems.
3. **Locks:** Locks can restrict physical access to systems and data. They can be mechanical or electronic and control access to doors, cabinets, and other secure areas.

Software access controls are logical controls that are used to restrict access to systems and data. Common examples of software access controls include:

1. **Passwords:** Passwords are the most common type of software access control. They authenticate users to systems and protect data from unauthorized access.
2. **Multi-factor authentication (MFA):** MFA adds an extra layer of security to systems and data by requiring users to provide additional authentication factors, such as a one-time code from their phone, in addition to their password.
3. **Access control lists (ACLs):** ACLs are lists of users or groups that are allowed or denied access to specific resources. ACLs can be used to control access to files, folders, networks, and other resources.

Technical access controls are an indispensable part of an organization's security posture. Through a combination of hardware and software mechanisms, these controls ensure that access to digital assets is tightly regulated and monitored. While hardware offers the tangible security mechanisms to protect and control access, software provides the sophisticated and adaptable solutions necessary to address the complexities of modern cyber threats.

C) Key Components of Logical Access Controls:

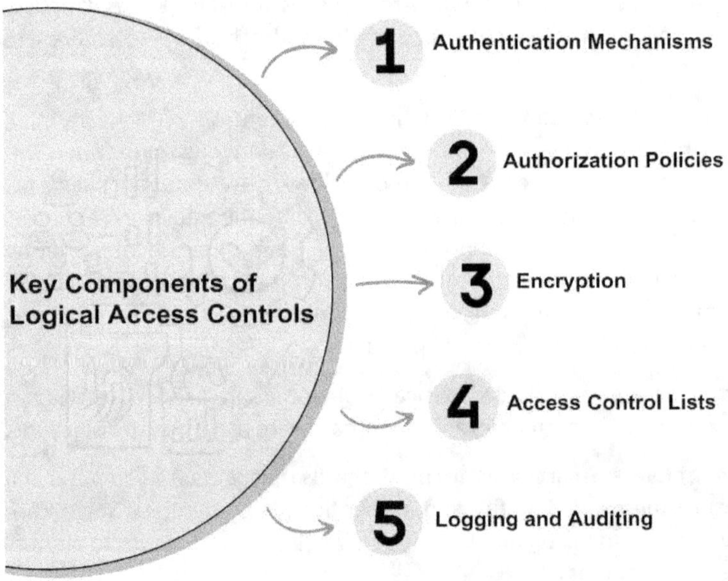

1. **Authentication Mechanisms:** Utilizing username-password combinations, multi-factor authentication, or biometric methods to validate the identity of users attempting to access a system.
2. **Authorization Policies:** Defining and enforcing permissions and privileges based on user roles or specific attributes. Authorization ensures that individuals have the appropriate level of access to perform their job functions.

3. **Encryption:** Employing encryption techniques to secure data during transmission and storage, preventing unauthorized interception and access.
4. **Access Control Lists (ACLs):** Configuring ACLs to specify which users or system processes are granted access to objects, as well as what operations are allowed on those given objects.
5. **Logging and Auditing:** Implementing logging mechanisms to record user activities and regularly auditing these logs to detect and respond to suspicious or unauthorized access attempts.

3.2.2 Principle of least privilege (PoLP)

This core concept advocates granting individuals or systems the minimum level of access or permissions necessary to perform their job functions. This approach minimizes the potential impact of security incidents and restricts unnecessary privileges. For example, a user who only needs to read emails should not be granted access to the company's customer database. Similarly, a user who only needs to deploy software to a single server should not be granted access to all of the company's servers.

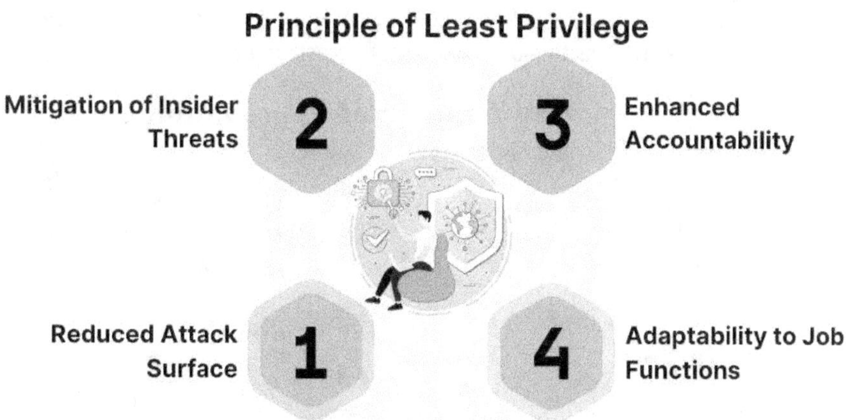

Key Aspects of the Principle of Least Privilege:

1. **Reduced Attack Surface:** By limiting access rights, the attack surface—areas vulnerable to exploitation—is minimized. This makes it more challenging for attackers to gain unauthorized access or compromise sensitive information.
2. **Mitigation of Insider Threats:** Insiders, intentionally or unintentionally, may pose security risks. Implementing the principle of least privilege mitigates the impact of insider threats by restricting the scope of potential malicious activities.
3. **Enhanced Accountability:** Assigning the minimum necessary privileges ensures more transparent accountability. In the event of a security incident, it becomes easier to trace the source and nature of unauthorized actions.

4. **Adaptability to Job Functions:** Tailoring access permissions to specific job roles ensures that individuals have the necessary tools and resources to fulfil their responsibilities without unnecessary privileges that could lead to security vulnerabilities.

The principle of least privilege is a vital cybersecurity principle that can help organizations to reduce the risk of data breaches, improve compliance, and reduce administrative overhead. By implementing the principle of least privilege, organizations can make it more difficult for attackers to exploit vulnerabilities and protect their data and systems.

3.2.3 Segregation of Duties (SoD)

SoD is a security principle that states that no single individual should have control over all aspects of a critical business process. This helps to reduce the risk of fraud and other malicious activity. It involves distributing tasks and privileges among multiple individuals or systems to prevent a single point of failure or compromise. This principle is vital in preventing conflicts of interest and unauthorized actions. For example, an employee who is responsible for creating new user accounts should not also be responsible for granting those accounts access to sensitive data or critical infrastructure.

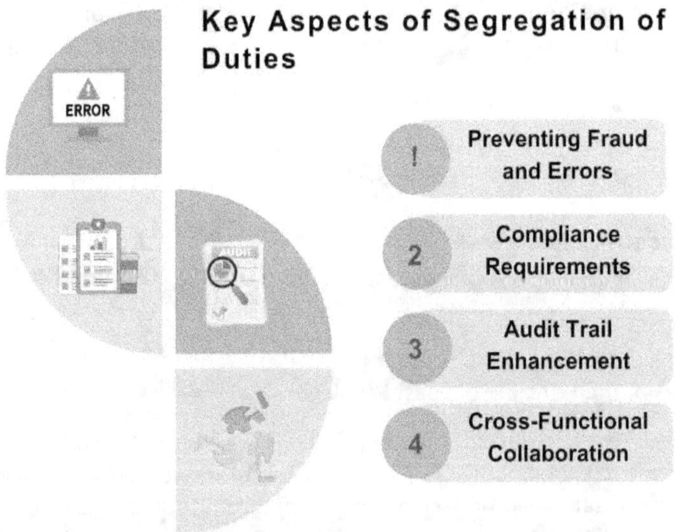

Key Aspects of Segregation of Duties:

1. **Preventing Fraud and Errors:** By dividing critical tasks among different individuals or systems, organizations reduce the risk of intentional or unintentional errors that could result in fraud, data loss, or other security incidents.

2. **Compliance Requirements:** Many regulatory frameworks and compliance standards mandate segregation of duties to ensure checks and balances. Adhering to SoD requirements helps organizations meet legal and regulatory obligations.
3. **Audit Trail Enhancement:** Segregation of duties contributes to the creation of a robust audit trail. When different individuals or systems are responsible for distinct tasks, it becomes easier to identify and investigate irregularities.
4. **Cross-Functional Collaboration:** SoD promotes collaboration and communication among different departments or teams. This collaboration helps in sharing insights, reducing silos, and fostering a culture of collective responsibility for security.

The principle of least privilege and segregation of duties are two important security principles that can help improve the effectiveness of logical access control systems. The effective implementation of logical access controls, the principle of least privilege, and segregation of duties can help organisations achieve optimal security necessary for compliance requirements.

Integration of Principle of least privilege (PoLP) & Segregation of Duties (SoD):

1. **Comprehensive Policies and Training:** Establish clear policies governing logical access controls and privileges. Regular training programs ensure that employees understand their responsibilities and the importance of security practices.
2. **Regular Audits and Reviews:** Conduct periodic audits to assess the effectiveness of access controls and SoD. Regular reviews help in identifying any deviations from established policies and correcting them promptly.
3. **Technology Integration:** Leverage technology solutions, such as identity and access management (IAM) systems, to automate and streamline the implementation of access controls, least privilege principles, and segregation of duties.
4. **Continuous Improvement:** Cyber threats evolve, and so should security practices. Establish a culture of continuous improvement by learning from security incidents, adapting policies accordingly, and staying abreast of emerging technologies and best practices.

3.3 Access Control Models

Access control refers to the mechanisms and policies that regulate access to physical and digital resources. Various types of access control are employed to ensure the confidentiality, integrity, and availability of sensitive information. Organizations must determine the appropriate access control model to adopt based on the type and sensitivity of data they're processing, organisation sector and compliance requirements. Here are some common types of access control:

Domain 3: Access Control Concepts

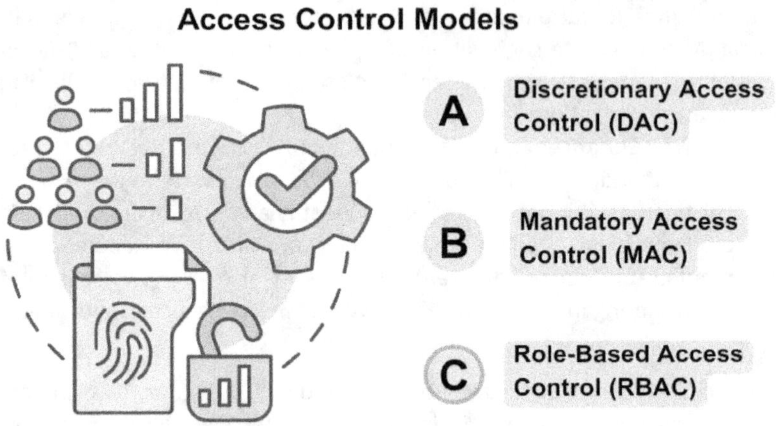

A) Discretionary Access Control (DAC):

In DAC model, the owner of a resource has the discretion to control access to that resource. The resource owner can set permissions for their files, folders, or systems, allowing or denying access to others. Discretionary access control (DAC) is like giving someone a key to a room, and the person who owns the room decides who gets the key. In DAC, the owner of something, like a computer file or a room, can say who can use it and who can't. This control is based on the idea that the owner of something can share it with others if they want to.

For example, think of a computer file. The person who made the file is like its owner. They can decide who can read, write, or change the file. When someone wants to use the file, they need to prove they have permission by showing their username and password, like showing an ID. In DAC, each thing (like a file) has an owner, and that owner decides who can use it. So, it's all about letting the owner choose who can get in or use their stuff. A simple example of DAC is how Unix computer systems work, where the owner of a file can say who can read, write, or run the file.

DAC attributes include:

1. The owner of the object may transfer object ownership to another user(s).
2. The owner may determine the access type of other users.
3. After certain attempts and authorization failures, the owner can restrict user access.
4. Unauthorized users are blind to object characteristics, such as file size, file name and directory path.
5. Object access is determined during access control list (ACL) authorization and based on user identification and/or group membership.

DAC is easy to implement and intuitive but has certain disadvantages, including:

1. Inherent vulnerabilities (Trojan horse)
2. Access Control List maintenance or capability

3. Grant and revoke permissions maintenance
4. Limited negative authorization power

DAC is often used in less restrictive environments where users have autonomy over their resources. It is the most common type of access control model used in operating systems and file systems, as well as in many other applications, such as databases and cloud storage services.

B) Mandatory Access Control (MAC):

In MAC, access control decisions are based on system-wide policies set by administrators. This is a method of limiting access to resources based on the sensitivity of the information that the resource contains and the authorization of the user to access information with that level of sensitivity. Organisation policies define the sensitivity of the resource by means of a security label. The security label is composed of a security level and zero or more security categories. The security level indicates a level or hierarchical classification of the information (for example, Restricted, Confidential, or Internal). The security category defines the category or group to which the information belongs (such as Project A or Project B). Users can access only the information in a resource to which their security labels entitle them. If the user's security label does not have enough authority, the user cannot access the information in the resource. Users and resources are assigned security labels or classifications, and access decisions are made based on these labels.

MAC is used widely in different sectors, which requires a system that can secure confidential data without constant supervision. It is mainly used in sectors like government offices, the military, health care, financial, and engineering projects.

The advantages of MAC are listed below:

1. High-level data protection (most secure system among roles, mandatory and discretionary systems): With MAC, one can be sure that their most confidential data is well protected and leaves no room for any leakage.
2. Centralized Information: Once data is set in a category, it cannot be de-categorized by anyone other than the head administrator. This makes the whole system centralized and under the control of only one authority.
3. Privacy: Data is set manually by an administrator. Only the admin can make changes to a category or the list of users' accesses to any category.

There are a few challenges with the MAC system. Such as the MAC system is not operationally flexible. It is not an easy task to initially input all data and create an ACL that won't create any trouble later. Also, MAC must be set up with good care as sometimes a piece of information needs to be shared among co-workers in the same organization, but MAC restricts anyone from doing so. Also the administration is required to put some consideration into the MAC system and ACL list now and then. Hence, MAC requires regular updating when new data is added or old data is deleted.

Domain 3: Access Control Concepts

C) Role-Based Access Control (RBAC):

RBAC is the most common access control model widely used in most organisations. Role-based access control (RBAC) restricts network access based on a person's role within an organization. Users are assigned roles based on their job functions or designations, and access privileges are associated with these roles. Employees are only allowed to access the information necessary to perform their job duties effectively. Access can be based on several factors, such as authority, responsibility, and job competency. In addition, access to computer resources can be limited to specific tasks, such as the ability to view, create, or modify a file.

Some of the designations in an RBAC tool can include:

1. Management role scope - it limits what objects the role group is allowed to manage.
2. Management role group - you can add and remove members.
3. Management role - these are the types of tasks that a specific role group, such as an administrator can perform.
4. Management role assignment – this links a role to a role group.

Advantages of RBAC are listed below:

1. Reduced Administrative Burden: RBAC simplifies administrative tasks and reduces the need for paperwork and frequent password changes when employees join, leave, or change roles. RBAC allows for quick role assignments that can be applied consistently across various systems and applications.
2. Enhanced Efficiency: RBAC provides a logical and streamlined approach to access control. Roles align with the organizational structure, allowing users to perform their tasks more efficiently and independently.
3. Improved Compliance: RBAC facilitates compliance by enabling IT departments and executives to manage how data is accessed and used. This is particularly valuable for industries like healthcare and finance, which handle sensitive data such as Protected Health Information (PHI) and Payment Card Industry (PCI) data.
4. Simplified Integration: RBAC eases the integration of third-party users into your network by assigning them predefined roles. This simplifies the onboarding process for external users, ensuring that they have access only to the necessary resources.

A core business function of any organization is protecting data. An RBAC system can ensure the company's information meets privacy and confidentiality regulations. Furthermore, it can secure key business processes, including access to IP, that affect the business from a competitive standpoint.

3.3.1 Other Access Control Models

Apart from the above-listed access control models, organisations can adopt other access control models to suit their needs. These models are:

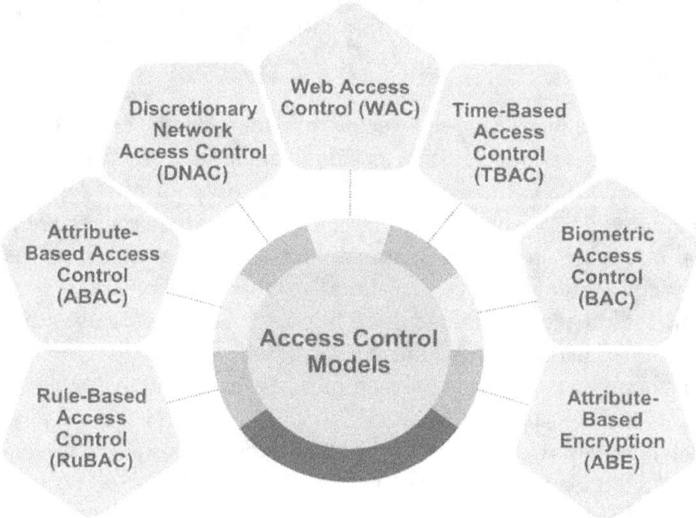

1. **Rule-Based Access Control (RuBAC):** RuBAC employs rules or policies to determine access permissions. These rules are often based on conditions, such as time of day, location, or specific user attributes. RuBAC allows for more dynamic and context-aware access control.
2. **Attribute-Based Access Control (ABAC):** ABAC uses attributes, such as user characteristics, resource attributes, and environmental conditions, to make access control decisions. It offers a fine-grained and flexible approach, allowing policies to be based on a wide range of attributes.
3. **Discretionary Network Access Control (DNAC):** DNAC focuses on controlling access to network resources. It allows network administrators to set policies that determine which users or devices can connect to the network and what level of access they have.
4. **Web Access Control (WAC):** WAC is specific to controlling access to web resources. It involves mechanisms for authentication, authorization, and sometimes accounting for users accessing web applications or services.
5. **Time-Based Access Control:** Time-based access control restricts access to resources based on specified time frames. For example, certain users may have access only during business hours, and outside those hours, access is restricted.
6. **Biometric Access Control:** Biometric access control uses physical or behavioral characteristics, such as fingerprints, iris scans, or facial

recognition, for authentication. Biometrics provide a high level of security by uniquely identifying individuals.

7. **Attribute-Based Encryption (ABE):** ABE is a cryptographic approach where access to encrypted data is based on attributes. Users are given cryptographic keys based on their attributes, and they can decrypt data if their attributes match the specified criteria.

A) Selection Factors:

1. **Choosing the Right Model:** Selecting the appropriate access control model depends on various factors, including organizational structure, security requirements, and the dynamic nature of access control needs.
2. **Flexibility:** DAC is suitable for environments where users require flexibility and autonomy in managing access controls. It is often employed in less restrictive settings, such as collaborative work environments.
3. **High-Security Environments:** MAC is ideal for environments with stringent security requirements, where a centralized and strictly enforced access control policy is necessary. Government agencies and military installations often leverage MAC.
4. **Scalability:** RBAC shines in organizations where roles align closely with job functions and where scalability is essential. It is adaptable to organizational changes and is widely used in enterprises of varying sizes.

B) Best Practices for Access Control:

Regardless of the chosen model, certain best practices apply to all access control implementation:

1. **Regular Audits:** Conduct periodic audits to ensure that access permissions align with organizational policies and that any deviations are promptly identified and addressed.
2. **User Education:** Educate users on access control policies and their responsibilities. A well-informed user base contributes to a security-conscious culture.
3. **Centralized Monitoring:** Implement centralized monitoring and logging mechanisms to track access events and detect anomalies or suspicious activities.
4. **Continuous Review:** Access control requirements evolve. Regularly review and update access control policies to adapt to changes in the organization's structure, technology, and security landscape.

Domain 4: Network Security

Network security is vital for maintaining the integrity and trustworthiness of networks and data. One important practice in this field is conducting network penetration tests, which are designed to evaluate system vulnerabilities and identify security weaknesses in servers, hosts, devices, and network services. While addressing digital vulnerabilities is critical, it is equally important to emphasize the physical security of network devices such as hubs, routers, and switches to prevent unauthorized access. Recent news highlights the increasing threat of cyberattacks targeting network infrastructure, underscoring the need for comprehensive security measures that encompass both digital and physical protections.

In the context of network security, it is easy to overlook the fact that a device without a visible data display does not guarantee protection against data capture or destruction at its access point. Despite the absence of a monitor through which users can directly view data, it remains imperative to recognize the potential risks associated with unsecured physical access points. Unauthorized individuals gaining physical access to network devices can pose significant threats. They may attempt to tamper with or manipulate the hardware, install malicious software, or extract sensitive information. By physically securing network devices, organizations can mitigate the risks of unauthorized access and protect the integrity, confidentiality, and availability of their networks.

Implementing measures such as locked cabinets, restricted access areas, and surveillance systems can help ensure that network devices remain physically safeguarded. Additionally, employing strict access control policies, such as granting permissions only to authorized personnel, further reinforces the security of the network infrastructure. By combining digital security measures with physical safeguards, organizations can establish a comprehensive network security strategy. This approach bolsters the overall resilience of the network, minimizes the potential for unauthorized breaches, and enhances the protection of valuable data assets.

Network security encompasses both digital and physical aspects. While conducting network penetration tests helps identify vulnerabilities in the digital realm, it is crucial to remember the importance of physically securing network devices to prevent unauthorized access and protect against potential risks. By adopting a holistic approach to network security, organizations can establish a robust defense against threats and maintain the usability and reliability of their networks and data.

4.1 Understand Computer Networking

A computer network is a set of communications channels that interconnects computing devices and enables them to exchange data electronically. In the simplest form of a network, a single client is connected to a single server where a client is a computing device such as a desktop PC, Laptop, or cell phone, which uses or consumes resources that are made available over a network. A server is a computing device that provides resources or services to other devices over a network. The true power of computer networks emerges when many computing devices can communicate with each other. For this reason, networks are typically characterized by many different clients being connected to many different servers. When discussing computer security in the context of networks, several other terms besides client and server are commonly used to describe different parts of a network.

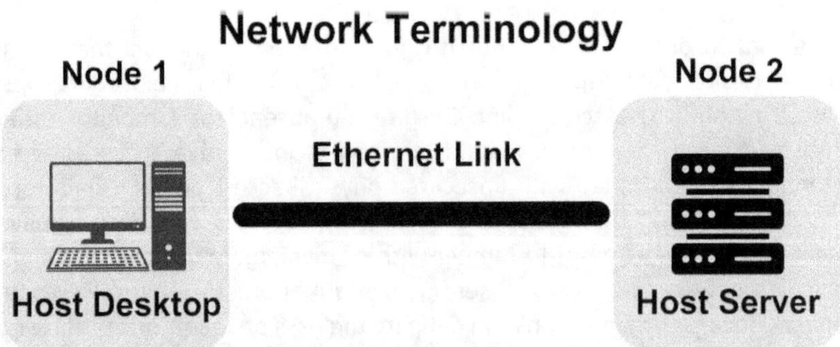

A) Network Terminology:

1. **Node:** A node that refers to a single conceptual computing device that is connected to the network. This could be a Desktop, Laptop, Mobile device, etc.

2. **Host:** This term refers to the actual physical computing device which resides at a node. Therefore, a node is more of a logical concept, while a host is more of a physical concept. It is important to note that computers are not the only possible hosts. Other physical devices connected to the network, such as routers and so forth, are also considered to be hosts.
3. **Link:** The term link refers to a connection between two hosts. As with the term node, the term link is more of a logical, abstract concept since, in reality, there are many different methods and communications media through which two hosts might be interconnected, such as physical cable, wireless or Bluetooth connection, etc.

B) Network Advantages:

Networks have become increasingly popular over the past several decades because they afford many advantages.

1. **Resource Sharing:** Allows common resources such as shared printers to be used efficiently.
2. Distribution of workload: a computational workload to be distributed across multiple machines.
3. **Increased Reliability:** A well-designed network can provide redundancy for many network resources.
4. **Expandability and Scalability:** Networks provide easy expandability and scalability. As their computational workload increases, organizations can often add additional nodes to the network to handle the increased demand for computational resources.

4.2 Open Systems Interconnection (OSI) model

The OSI (Open Systems Interconnection) model is a fundamental framework for understanding and implementing network protocols and architecture. Comprising seven distinct layers, the ISO model plays a crucial role in the study of networks and network security, offering several key advantages and benefits.

First and foremost, the OSI layers provide a standardized approach to network communication. Each layer has specific functions and responsibilities, ensuring clear separation of tasks and facilitating interoperability between different network devices and technologies. This standardization simplifies network design, implementation, and troubleshooting, allowing for greater efficiency and effectiveness in managing networks. Also, the ISO model serves as a conceptual model, aiding in the comprehension and analysis of complex network systems. By dividing the network into layers, it becomes easier to understand the flow of data, identify potential bottlenecks, and pinpoint areas of vulnerability. This holistic view enables network administrators and security professionals to develop robust strategies to protect against threats and ensure the integrity, confidentiality, and availability of network resources. In the realm of network security, the ISO model proves invaluable. Each layer contributes to safeguarding the network from various risks and attacks. For instance, the lower layers (Physical, Data Link, and Network) establish secure connections, implement access controls, and manage routing protocols. Meanwhile, the upper layers (Transport, Session, Presentation, and Application) focus on encryption, authentication, and the secure exchange of data.

By understanding the ISO layers, network professionals gain the ability to analyze network vulnerabilities comprehensively. They can identify weak points at different layers, implement appropriate security measures, and enforce best practices to mitigate risks effectively. This knowledge empowers individuals to design and manage secure networks, ensuring the protection of sensitive information, preventing unauthorized access, and maintaining business continuity.

The ISO layer plays a pivotal role in learning networks and network security. Its standardized framework, conceptual model, and security considerations provide a solid foundation for understanding, designing, and securing networks. By studying and implementing the ISO layers, network professionals can enhance their expertise, optimize network performance, and fortify defenses against cyber threats. Let us have a close look at the seven OSI layers.

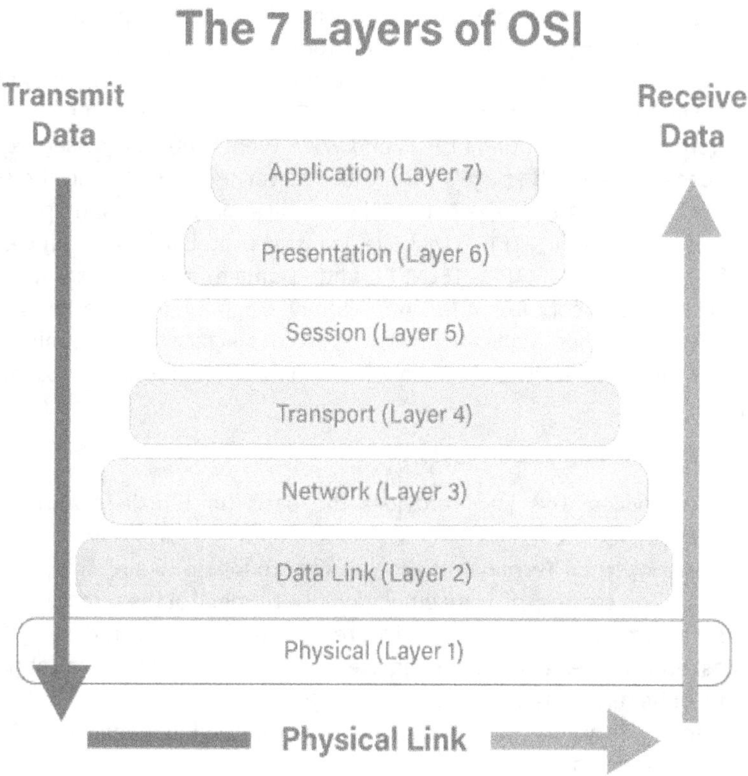

The seven layers of OSI and their description are as below.

4.2.1 Layer 7: Application Layer

This is the only layer that directly interacts with data from the user. Software applications like web browsers and email clients rely on the application layer to initiate communications. Client software applications are not part of the application layer; rather the application layer is responsible for the protocols and data handling that the software relies on to present meaningful data to the user. Application layer protocols include HTTP as well as SMTP (Simple Mail Transfer Protocol is the protocol that enables email communications).

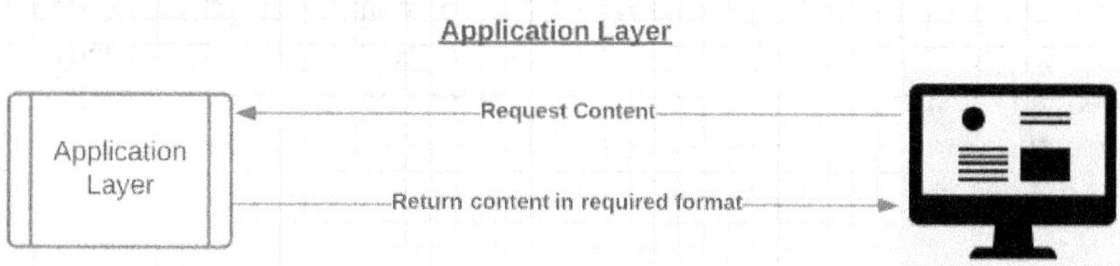

Handling of data in various ways occurs in this layer, enabling users or software to access the network. Some services provided by this layer include email, file transfers, distributing results to users, directory services, and network resources. The Application Layer contains a variety of protocols that users commonly utilize. One widely-used application protocol is HTTP (Hypertext Transfer Protocol), which forms the foundation of the World Wide Web. When a browser requests a web page, it sends the page's URL to the server using HTTP, and the server responds by sending the page back. Other application protocols in use include File Transfer Protocol (FTP), Trivial File Transfer Protocol (TFTP), Simple Mail Transfer Protocol (SMTP), TELNET, and Domain Name System (DNS). Additionally, protocols like APIs (Application Programming Interfaces), XML gateways, and other application-related protocols facilitate communication between different software systems and enable integration across diverse platforms.

Functions of the Application Layer:

1. **Mail Services:** This layer provides the basis for E-mail forwarding and storage.
2. **Network Virtual Terminal:** It allows a user to log on to a remote host. The application creates software emulation of a terminal at the remote host. The user's computer talks to the software terminal, which in turn talks to the host and vice versa. Then, the remote host believes it is communicating with one of its terminals and allows the user to log on.
3. **Directory Services:** This layer provides access to global information about various services.
4. **File Transfer, Access, and Management (FTAM):** FTAM is a standard mechanism for accessing and managing files. Users can access and manage files on a remote computer and retrieve files from that computer.

4.2.2 Layer 6: Presentation Layer

The primary goal of this layer is to take care of the syntax and semantics of the information exchanged between two communicating systems. The presentation layer ensures that the data is sent in such a way that the receiver will understand the data and will be able to use the data. Languages (syntax) can be different in the two communicating systems. Under this condition presentation layer plays the role of translator. To make it possible for computers with different data representations to communicate, the data structures to be exchanged can be defined abstractly. The presentation layer manages these abstract data structures and allows higher-level data structures (e.g., accounting records) to be defined and exchanged.

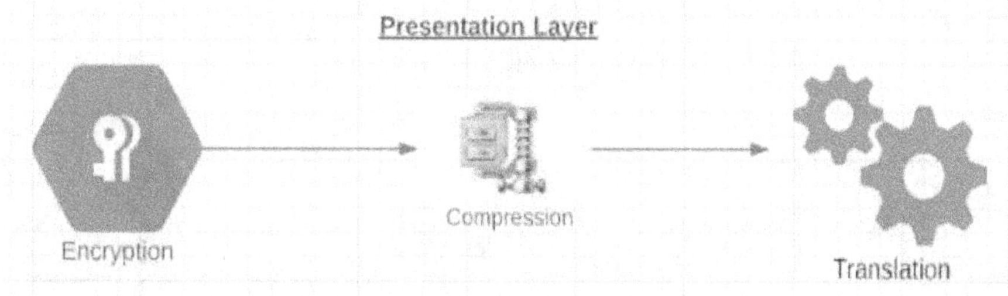

Functions of Presentation Layer:

1. **Translation:** Before being transmitted, information in the form of characters and numbers should be changed to bit streams. The presentation layer is responsible for the ability of computer systems or software to exchange data and use information between encoding methods, as different computers use different encoding methods. It translates data between the formats the network requires and the format of the computer.
2. **Encryption:** It carries out encryption at the transmitter end and decryption at the receiver end.
3. **Compression:** It carries out data compression of the data to be transmitted to reduce the bandwidth. The primary role of Data compression is to reduce the number of bits to be transmitted over a network. Due to their higher sizes, it is important in transmitting multimedia such as audio, video, text, etc.

4.2.3 Layer 5: Session Layer

This is the layer responsible for opening and closing communication between the two devices. The time between when the communication is opened and closed is known as the session. The session layer ensures that the session stays open long enough to transfer all the data being exchanged and then promptly closes the session to avoid wasting resources. The session layer also synchronizes data transfer with checkpoints. For example, if a 100-megabyte file is being transferred, the session layer could set a checkpoint every 5 megabytes. In the case of a disconnect or a crash, after 52 megabytes have been transferred, the session could be resumed from the last checkpoint, meaning only the remaining 50 megabytes of data need to be transferred. Without the checkpoints, the entire transfer would have to begin again from scratch.

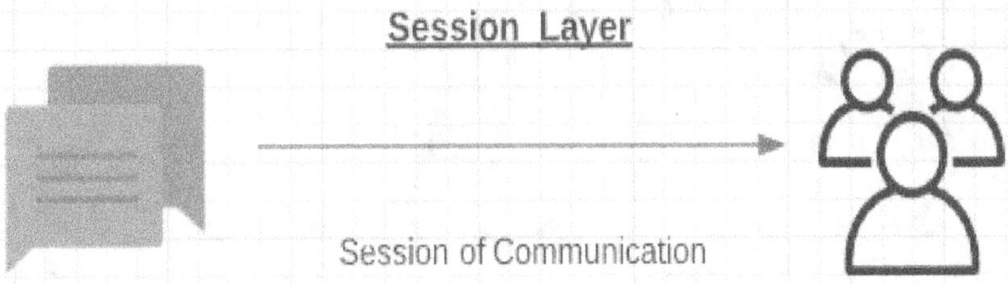

The Session Layer allows users on different machines to establish active communication sessions between them. Its main aim is to establish, maintain and synchronize the interaction between communicating systems. The session layer manages and synchronizes the conversation between two different applications. In the Session layer, streams of data are marked and are resynchronized properly, so that the ends of the messages are not cut prematurely and data loss is avoided.

Functions of Session Layer:

1. **Dialog Control:** This layer allows two systems to start communicating in either half-duplex or full-duplex mode.
2. **Token Management:** This layer prevents two parties from attempting the same critical operation at the same time.
3. **Synchronization:** This layer allows a process to add checkpoints that are considered synchronization points in a stream of data. Example: If a system is sending a file of 80 pages, adding checkpoints after every five pages is recommended. This ensures that the 5-page unit is successfully received and acknowledged. This is beneficial at the time of crash as if a crash happens at page number 69; there is no need to retransmit 1 to 65 pages.

4.2.4 Layer 4: Transport Layer

This layer is responsible for end-to-end communication between the two devices. This includes taking data from the session layer and breaking it up into chunks called segments before sending it to layer 3. The transport layer on the receiving device is responsible for re-assembling the segments into data so that the session layer can process it further. The transport layer is also responsible for flow control and error control. Flow control determines an optimal speed of transmission to ensure that a sender with a fast connection doesn't overwhelm a receiver with a slow connection. The transport layer performs error control on the receiving end by ensuring that the data received is complete and requesting retransmission if it isn't.

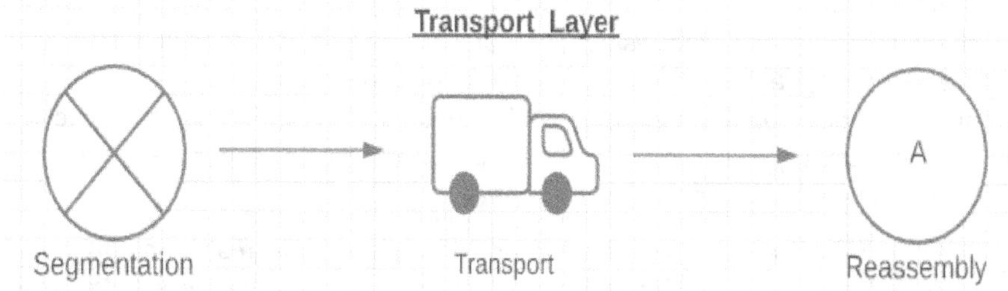

The primary function of the Transport layer is to accept data from the layer above, split it up into smaller units, pass these data units to the Network layer, and ensure that all the pieces arrive correctly at the other end. Furthermore, all this must be done efficiently and in a way that isolates the upper layers from the inevitable changes in the hardware technology. The Transport layer also determines what type of service to provide to the Session layer and, ultimately, to the users of the network. The most popular type of transport connection is a point-to-point channel that delivers error-free messages or bytes in the order in which they were sent. The Transport layer is an actual end-to-end layer, all the way from the source to the destination. In other words, a program on the source machine carries on a conversation with a similar program on the destination machine, using the message headers and control messages.

Functions of Transport Layer:

1. **Service Point Addressing:** The transport Layer header includes the service point address, which is a port address. This layer gets the message to the correct process on the computer, unlike the Network Layer, which gets each packet to the correct computer.
2. **Segmentation and Reassembling:** A message is divided into segments; each segment contains a sequence number, which enables this layer to reassemble the message. The message is reassembled correctly upon arrival at the destination and replaces packets that were lost in transmission.
3. **Connection Control:** It includes two types:
    - **Connectionless Transport Layer:** Each segment is considered as an independent packet and delivered to the transport layer at the destination machine.
    - **Connection-Oriented Transport Layer:** Before delivering packets, a connection is made with the transport layer at the destination device.
4. **Flow Control:** In this layer, flow control is performed end to end.
5. **Error Control:** Error Control is performed end to end in this layer to ensure that the complete message arrives at the receiving transport layer without any error. Error Correction is done through retransmission.

4.2.5 Layer 3: Network Layer

The network layer facilitates data transfer between two different networks. It breaks up segments from the transport layer into smaller units, called packets, on the sender's device and reassembles these packets on the receiving device. The network layer also finds the best physical path for the data to reach its destination, which is known as routing.

The network Layer controls the operation of the subnet. Its main aim is to deliver packets from source to destination across multiple links (networks). This layer routes the signal through different channels to the other end and acts as a network controller. It also divides the outgoing messages into packets and assembles incoming packets into messages for higher layers. In broadcast networks, the routing problem is simple, so the network layer is often thin or even non-existent.

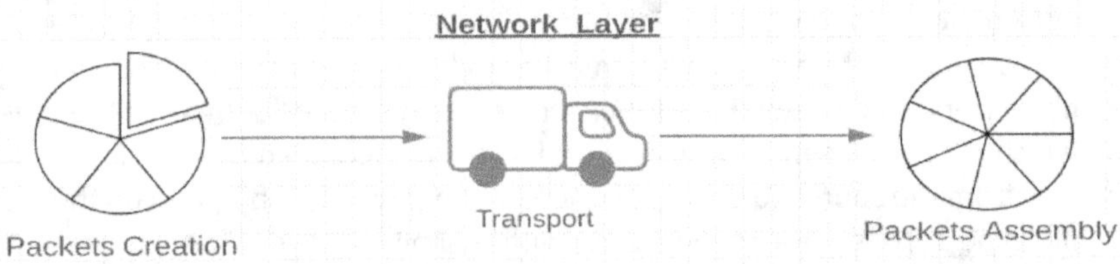

Functions of Network Layer:

1. **Routing**: Responsible for finding the best physical path for the data to reach its destination. Routers and gateways operate in the layer. Network Layer provides the mechanism for routing the packets on their way to the destination.
2. **Logical Addressing**: This layer implements logical addressing. It adds a header to the packet, which includes the logical addresses of both the sender and the receiver.
3. **Internetworking**: The primary role of the network layer is to provide logical connections between different types of networks.
4. **Fragmentation**: Fragmentation is a process of breaking the packets into the most minor individual data units that travel through different networks.

4.2.6 Layer 2: Data Link Layer

The data link layer ensures reliable node-to-node data transfer. It creates frames from network layer packets and passes them to the physical layer for transmission. It also synchronizes the data and handles error detection and correction using error detection bits. The encoded data is then sent to the physical layer. Outgoing messages are assembled into frames, and the system waits for acknowledgments after transmission. Its main goal is to turn raw transmission into a line that appears free of undetected errors to the network layer. It does this by breaking data into frames, usually a few hundred or thousand bytes, and sending them sequentially. If the service is reliable, the receiver confirms correct receipt by sending back an acknowledgment frame.

The data link layer is very similar to the network layer, except the data link layer facilitates data transfer between two devices on the SAME network. The data link layer takes packets from the network layer and breaks them into smaller pieces called frames. Like the network layer, the data link layer is also responsible for flow control and error control in intra-network communication (The transport layer only does flow control and error control for inter-network communications).

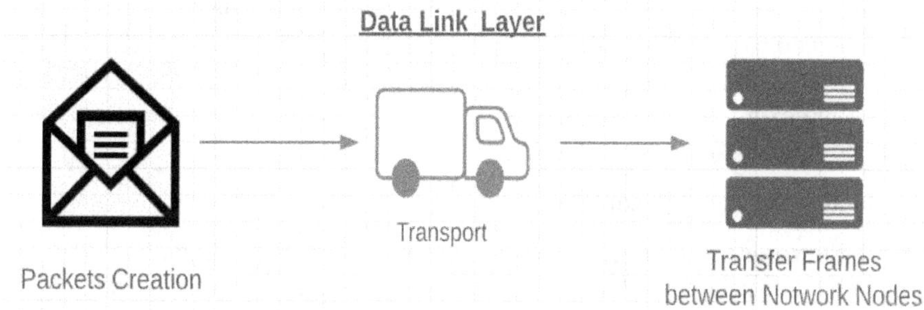

Functions of Data Link Layer:

1. **Framing:** Frames are the streams of bits received from the network layer divided into manageable data units by the Data Link Layer.
2. **Physical Addressing:** The Data Link layer adds a header to the frame to define the physical address of the sender or receiver of the frame if the frames are to be distributed to different systems on the network.
3. **Flow Control:** Flow control provides a mechanism to prevent a fast transmitter from running a slow receiver by buffering the extra bit. This prevents traffic jams on the receiver side.
4. **Error Control:** This mechanism prevents frame duplication and achieves error control by adding a trailer at the end of the frame.
5. **Access Control:** Protocols of this layer determine which device has control over the link when two or more devices are connected to the same link.

4.2.7 Layer 1: Physical Layer

The physical layer is the lowest layer of the OSI reference model. It is responsible for sending bits from one computer to another. This layer is not concerned with the meaning of the bits but with setting up a physical connection to the network and transmitting and receiving signals.

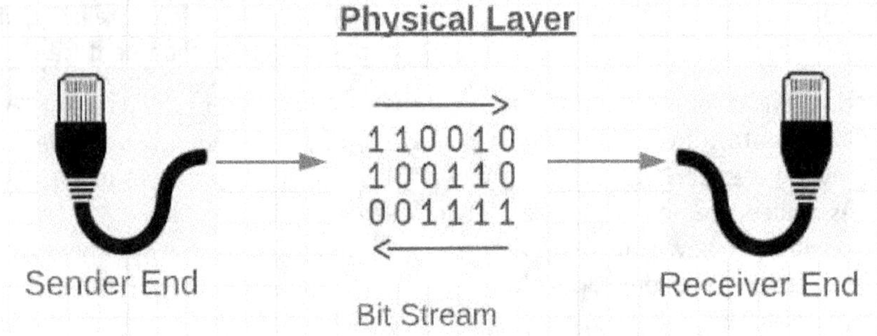

This layer includes the physical equipment involved in the data transfer, such as cables and switches. It is also the layer where the data gets converted into a bit stream, which is a string of 1s and 0s. The physical layers of both devices must also agree on a signal convention so that the 1s can be distinguished from the 0s on both devices.

Functions of the Physical Layer:

1. **Representation of Bits:** Data in this layer consists of a stream of bits. The bits must be encoded into signals for transmission. This layer defines the type of encoding, i.e., how 0s and 1s are changed to signals.
2. **Data Rate:** This layer defines the rate of transmission which is the number of bits per second.
3. **Synchronization:** This deals with the synchronization of the transmitter and receiver, which are synchronized at the bit level.
4. **Interface:** The physical layer defines the transmission interface between devices and the transmission medium.
5. **Line Configuration:** This layer connects devices with the medium: Point-to-Point configuration and Multipoint configuration.
6. **Topologies:** Devices must be connected using the following topologies: Mesh, Star, Ring, and Bus.
7. **Transmission Modes:** The Physical Layer defines the direction of transmission between two devices: Simplex, Half-Duplex, and Full-Duplex. Deals with baseband and broadband transmission.

4.3 Internet Protocol

In the realm of networking, a protocol serves as a universally accepted method for executing specific tasks and structuring data to enable effective communication and mutual comprehension between two or more devices. To comprehend the necessity of protocols, let's draw a parallel with the process of sending a letter. When addressing an envelope, there's a prescribed sequence: name, street address, city, state, and zip code. If, however, an envelope is placed in a mailbox with the zip code leading the way, followed by the street address, state, and so forth, the postal service would not be able to deliver it. The reason behind this seamless postal system is a mutually agreed-upon protocol for address formatting. In much the same manner, all IP data packets must adhere to specific guidelines regarding the arrangement of information in a particular sequence, and all IP addresses must conform to a standardized structure to ensure efficient communication within the network.

Two Most Relevant IP Protocols

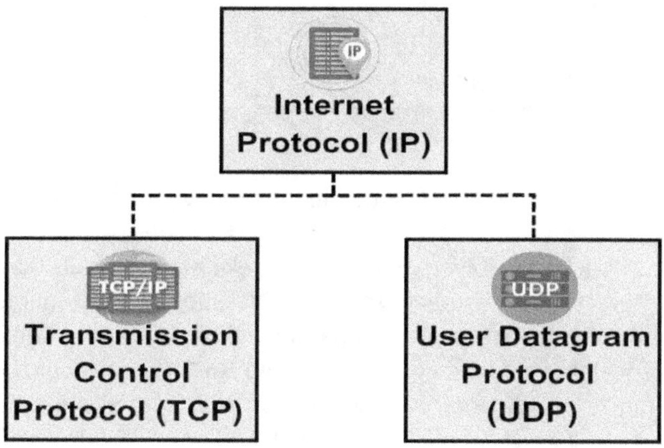

The Internet Protocol (IP) serves as a set of rules or protocols governing the routing and addressing of data packets, ensuring their proper travel across networks to reach the designated destination. As data journeys through the Internet, it is segmented into smaller units known as packets. Each packet is accompanied by IP information crucial for routers to accurately route them to their intended locations. Every device or domain connected to the Internet possesses a unique IP address, and the association of packets with their respective IP addresses ensures that data reaches its intended destination. Upon reaching their destinations, packets undergo distinct handling processes based on the specific transport protocol used in conjunction with IP. The two most prevalent transport protocols are Transmission Control Protocol (TCP) and User Datagram Protocol (UDP). These protocols determine how data is managed, ensuring reliable and orderly communication in the case of TCP, or faster but potentially less reliable communication in the case of UDP.

4.3.1 Internet Protocol version 4 (IPv4)

IPv4, the fourth version of the Internet Protocol, stands as a widely adopted protocol for data communication across various network types globally. It functions as a connectionless protocol within packet-switched layer networks, like Ethernet, establishing a logical connection between network devices. This protocol assigns a unique identification to each device called as IP address. This address facilitates seamless communication. There are many ways to configure IPv4 with all kinds of devices – including manual and automatic configurations – depending on the network type.

IP Address: An IP address is a unique identifier assigned to a device or domain that connects to the Internet. Each IP address is a series of characters, such as '192.168.1.1'. Via DNS resolvers, which translate human-readable domain names into IP addresses, users are able to access websites without memorizing this complex series of characters. Each IP packet will contain both the IP address of the device or domain sending the packet and the IP address of the intended recipient, much like how both the destination address and the return address are included on a piece of mail. The fourth version of IP (IPv4 for short) was introduced in 1983. However, just as there are only so many possible permutations for automobile license plate numbers, and they have to be reformatted periodically, the supply of available IPv4 addresses has become depleted.

IPv4 uses 32-bit addresses for Ethernet communication in five classes: A, B, C, D, and E. Classes A, B, and C have different bit lengths for addressing the network host. Class D addresses are reserved for multicasting, while class E addresses are reserved for future use. Class A has a subnet mask 255.0.0.0 or /8, B has a subnet mask 255.255.0.0 or /16 and class C has a subnet mask 255.255.255.0 or /24. For example, with a /16 subnet mask, the network 192.168.0.0 may use the address range of 192.168.0.0 to 192.168.255.255. Network hosts can take any address from this range; however, the address 192.168.255.255 is reserved for broadcast within the network. The maximum number of host addresses IPv4 can assign to end users is 232.

Comments on class visibility and usage:

Public classes: These should be used for core functionalities, such as defining IPv4 address classes and subnet calculations, to allow access across different parts of a program.

Private classes: Internal utility classes, such as those handling address parsing, validation, or subnet calculations, should be marked private to encapsulate implementation details and prevent misuse outside their scope.

Usage: Public classes can be used in APIs or modules where external access is needed, while private classes are suitable for internal processing within the module or class.

4.3.2 Internet Protocol version 6 (IPv6)

IPv6, the sixth version of the Internet Protocol, emerges as a cutting-edge protocol designed to overcome the limitations of its predecessor, IPv4. It is rapidly gaining prominence as a global standard for data communication across diverse network types. Operating as a connectionless protocol within packet-switched layer networks, IPv6, like Ethernet, facilitates a logical connection between network devices. One of its distinctive features is the substantial expansion of the address space, addressing the challenges of IPv4 address exhaustion.

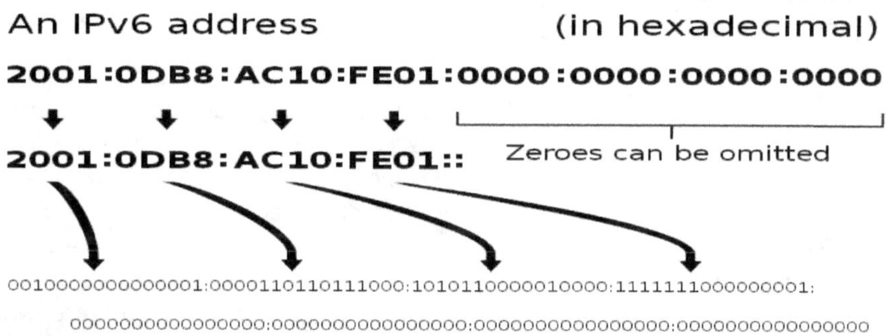

IP Address in IPv6: An IP address in IPv6, much like in IPv4, serves as a unique identifier assigned to devices or domains connected to the Internet. Unlike the 32-bit addresses in IPv4, IPv6 utilizes 128-bit addresses, represented in hexadecimal format. An example of an IPv6 address is '2001:0db8:85a3:0000:0000:8a2e:0370:7334'. IPv6 addresses are designed to accommodate the growing number of connected devices and to offer a vastly expanded address space.

IPv6 introduces advancements in network architecture, including the simplification of address configuration through Stateless Address Autoconfiguration (SLAAC) and the integration of security features, such as IPsec, as a fundamental component of the protocol. As with IPv4, users can access websites via DNS resolvers, translating human-readable domain names into IPv6 addresses.

IPv6 utilizes a different addressing structure, employing eight groups of four hexadecimal digits, separated by colons. The larger address space allows for greater flexibility and scalability in network design. Subnetting in IPv6 is expressed through CIDR notation, and its subnet masks are represented as prefixes. For example, a subnet with a prefix length of /64 would have an address range from '2001:0db8:85a3:0000:0000:0000:0000:0000' to '2001:0db8:85a3:ffff:ffff:ffff:ffff:ffff'.

As the demand for IP addresses continues to escalate, IPv6 serves as the forward-looking solution, providing the necessary infrastructure to accommodate the growing number of devices and ensuring the continued expansion and resilience of the internet.

4.4 Wireless Fidelity (Wi-Fi)

Wi-Fi is a wireless networking technology that uses radio waves to connect devices to the Internet. It is the most common type of wireless network in use today, and it is used in homes, businesses, and public places around the world. It relies on radio waves to transmit data between devices, allowing for seamless communication and providing the convenience of internet access without physical constraints.

Wi-Fi operates based on the IEEE 802.11 family of standards, each letter denoting a different version or amendment. Common standards include 802.11a, 802.11b, 802.11g, 802.11n, 802.11ac, and the latest, 802.11ax (Wi-Fi 6) each with its own strengths and weaknesses. These standards dictate the frequency bands, data transfer rates, and other technical specifications that ensure compatibility and performance across Wi-Fi-enabled devices. Wi-Fi protocols operate in two primary frequency bands: 2.4 GHz and 5 GHz. The 2.4 GHz band offers better coverage but may experience more interference, while the 5 GHz band provides faster speeds with less interference but has a shorter range. Dual-band routers and devices can operate in both bands, balancing coverage and performance. Multiple Input Multiple Output (MIMO) is a technology employed in modern Wi-Fi standards like 802.11n and 802.11ac. It involves multiple antennas on both the router and the device, enabling simultaneous data transmission and reception, thereby enhancing data throughput and overall network performance.

4.4.1 Wi-Fi Protocols

1. **802.11a:** This protocol operates in the 5 GHz frequency band and offers the highest speeds of any Wi-Fi protocol, but it has a shorter range than other protocols.
2. **802.11b:** This wireless standard operates in the 2.4 GHz frequency band and has a longer range than 802.11a, but it offers slower speeds.
3. **802.11g:** This wireless standard operates in the 2.4 GHz frequency band and offers speeds that are faster than 802.11b but not as fast as 802.11a.
4. **802.11n:** This wireless standard operates in both the 2.4 GHz and 5 GHz frequency bands and offers speeds that are faster than 802.11g.
5. **802.11ac:** It operates in the 5 GHz frequency band and offers speeds that are significantly faster than 802.11n.
6. **802.11ax (Wi-Fi 6):** This technology operates in both the 2.4 GHz and 5 GHz frequency bands and offers speeds significantly faster than 802.11ac, as well as improved performance in crowded environments.

4.4.2 Wi-Fi-Security

Wi-Fi security is important because it protects your network from unauthorized access.

A) Encryption:

1. **Wired Equivalent Privacy (WEP):** WEP is the oldest Wi-Fi security protocol and is no longer considered to be secure.
2. **Wi-Fi Protected Access (WPA):** WPA is a more secure protocol than WEP, but it is also vulnerable to attack.
3. **Wi-Fi Protected Access 2 (WPA2):** WPA2 is the most secure Wi-Fi security protocol in use today.
4. **Wi-Fi Protected Access 3 (WPA3):** The latest advancement in Wi-Fi security, WPA3, addresses vulnerabilities in WPA2. It enhances encryption and strengthens protection against brute-force attacks.

B) Authentication Mechanisms:

1. **Pre-Shared Key (PSK):** Commonly used in home networks, PSK requires users to enter a passphrase for authentication.
2. **Enterprise Authentication:** For a higher level of security, enterprise-level authentication methods such as 802.1X and EAP (Extensible Authentication Protocol) are preferred in business environments.
3. **Hidden SSID:** Service Set Identifier (SSID) is the network name broadcasted by the router, usually visible to every wireless device in the vicinity. While hiding the SSID may seem like an additional layer of security, it's considered a minimal deterrent, as determined attackers can still discover the network through various means.

4. **MAC Address Filtering:** This security measure involves allowing only specific devices identified by their MAC addresses to connect to the Wi-Fi network. However, MAC addresses can be spoofed, making this method less foolproof.
5. **Regular Firmware Updates:** It is essential to keep Wi-Fi routers' firmware up-to-date. Manufacturers release updates to patch security vulnerabilities and improve overall performance.

C) Best Practices for Wi-Fi Security:

1. **Strong Passwords:** Use complex and unique passwords for Wi-Fi networks, combining uppercase and lowercase letters, numbers, and symbols.
2. **Regular Security Audits:** Perform periodic security audits to identify and rectify potential vulnerabilities in the Wi-Fi network.
3. **Network Segmentation:** Separate the network into segments to contain potential breaches, especially in business environments. Guest networks should be isolated from critical systems.
4. **Disable Unnecessary Services:** If not in use, turn off unnecessary features like WPS (Wi-Fi Protected Setup), as they can introduce additional security risks.
5. **Monitor Network Activity:** Utilize network monitoring tools to track and analyze network activity, identifying anomalies or suspicious behavior.

4.5 Port Scanning

A computer hardware port is a connection point or interface between a computer and an external or internal physical device. Internal ports may connect such devices as hard drives and CD ROM or DVD drives; external ports may connect modems, printers, mice, and other devices. These are physical. E.g. Serial Port, Parallel Port, SCSI Port, USB Port, etc.

In computer networking, a port is a communication endpoint. At the software level, within an operating system, a port is a logical construct that identifies a specific process or a type of network service. A port is a virtual point where network connections start and end. Ports are software-based and managed by a computer's operating system. A port number is always associated with an IP address of a host and the type of transport protocol used for communication. Each port is associated with a specific process or service. Ports allow computers to easily differentiate between different kinds of traffic. E.g. emails go to an SMTP port 25, Webpages go to an HTTP Port 80 and HTTPS uses port 443. Etc

A port scanner is a software program that is designed to examine the hosts which reside at IP addresses and record which ports are open on each host along with which known vulnerabilities are present. For network architecture or a Cyber security analyst port scanners can be extremely valuable. These port scanners can provide a useful way of identifying and evaluating the strengths and weaknesses of a network. The same port scanner information can be used by a network administrator or Cyber security analyst to evaluate the security of a network. It can also be used by Cybercriminals to identify network weaknesses or to assess how or at which point to attack a network. Now a day's high-quality port scanner software is freely available online for Cyber Security engineers and Cybercriminals. As with so many other tools that exist online; port scanners can be used with good intentions or can be used to cause harm depending upon the goal of the user who possesses the tool.

A port scanner is a simple computer program that checks all of those ports – and responds with one of three possible responses: Open, Closed, or Filtered. There are two kinds of ports on each computer – TCP, and UDP – and 65,536 of each. The first 1024 TCP ports are well-known ports like FTP(21), HTTP(80), or SSH(22). Anything above 1024 is available for use by services or applications.

Port Scanning

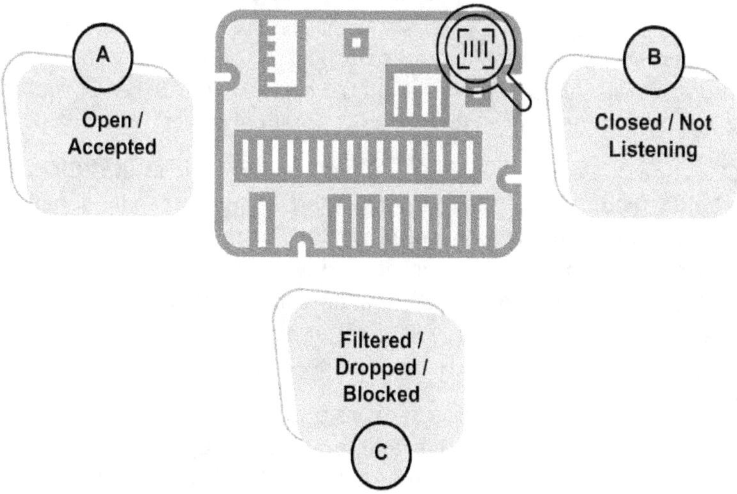

Port scanning is quite simple: a port scanner sends a request to connect to a port on a computer and records the response. There are three possible responses:

A) **Open / Accepted:** The computer responds and asks if there is anything it can do in response.
B) **Closed / Not Listening:** The computer responds "This port is currently in use and unavailable at this time."
C) **Filtered / Dropped / Blocked:** The computer doesn't even respond to these requests.

Cybercriminals are looking for open ports that they can use as communication relays or penetration vectors into a network. Any open port they can find is a possible access point for further infiltration into the network.

4.5.1 Port Scanning Techniques

A) Ping Scan: The most straightforward port scans are ping scans. A ping is an Internet Control Message Protocol (ICMP) echo request – attackers are looking for any ICMP reply, which indicates that the target is alive. A ping scan is an automated blast of many ICMP echo requests to different targets to see who responds. Administrators usually disable ping either on the firewall or on the router. It's quick and easy to turn off this functionality and make it impossible to scout the network this way. However, ping is a good troubleshooting tool, and turning it off makes tracking down network problems a little more complicated.

B) TCP Half-Open: One of the more common and popular port scanning techniques is the TCP Half-Open port scan, sometimes referred to as SYN scan. It's a fast and sneaky scan that tries to find potential open ports on the target computer. This scan is fast because it never completes the full TCP 3-way handshake. The scanner sends a SYN message and notes the SYN-ACK responses. The scanner doesn't complete the connection by sending the final ACK; it leaves the target hanging. Any SYN-ACK responses are possible connections: an RST(reset) response means the port is closed, but there is a live computer here. No responses indicate SYN is filtered on the network. Any SYN-ACK replies are a quick way cybercriminals can find the next potential target.

C) TCP Connect: This port scanning technique is the same as the TCP Half-Open scan, but instead of leaving the target hanging, the port scanner completes the TCP connection. It's not as popular a technique as the TCP Half-Open. First, the attacker has to send one more packet per scan, which increases the amount of traffic the attacker is causing on the network. Second, since the attacker completes the connection with the target, it might trip an alarm that the Half-Open scan wouldn't.

D) UDP Connect: When the attacker runs a UDP port scan, he sends either an empty packet or a packet that has a different payload per port, depending on the attacker's purpose. The trick with a UDP scan is that the attacker will only get a response if the port is closed, which means the attacker might know that there is a computer there. Depending on which port responded attacker might know that it has DNS or SNMP running, but that's pretty much it. No response means that either the port is open or it's filtered, and the attacker might have to run the scan more than once before he figures anything out about the target. An attacker could be waiting a while to get a response that might never come. One more logical use of a UDP scan is to send a DNS request to UDP port 53 and see if he gets a DNS reply. If the attacker does get a reply, then he knows that there is a DNS server on that computer. A UDP scan can be useful to scout for active services that way, and the Nmap port scanner is preconfigured to send requests for many standard services.

E) Stealth Scanning: Sometimes an attacker wants to run a port scan that is even quieter and less obvious than the other kinds of scans. Thankfully, TCP includes some flags that allow attackers to do just that. When an attacker sends a port scan with a packet and the FIN flag, the attacker is sending the packet and not expecting a response. If he does get an RST he can assume that the port is closed. If he gets nothing back that indicates the port is open. Firewalls are looking for SYN packets, so FIN packets slip through undetected. The X-MAS scan sends a packet with the FIN, URG, and PUSH flags and expects an RST or no response, just like the FIN scan. There isn't much practical use for this scan, but it does make the packet resemble a Christmas tree. The attacker can also send packets with no flags, called a NULL packet, and the response is either an RST or nothing. The good thing – for the hacker – about these scans is that they don't usually show up in logs. More recent Intrusion Detection Software (IDS) and WireShark tool will catch these scans. If the target is a Microsoft OS, the attacker will only see closed ports – but if the attacker does find an open port, he can assume that it's not a Windows machine. The most significant advantage of using these flags is that they can slip past the firewall, which makes the results more reliable. Port scanning and penetration testing are essential parts of the cyber kill chain that can lead to intrusion, exploitation, privilege escalation, and more. Port scanning is often just one part of the bigger picture in a cyber-attack.

4.6 Understanding Network Threats and Attacks

Network security involves an in-depth analysis of how networks are targeted and attacked. By delving into the techniques and strategies employed by malicious actors, we gain valuable insights into vulnerabilities and potential threats. This knowledge enables us to develop robust defense mechanisms and safeguard networks against sophisticated attacks.

Network Vulnerabilities: Networks provide many advantages. However, they also have several characteristics that make them vulnerable to attacks by Cybercriminals.

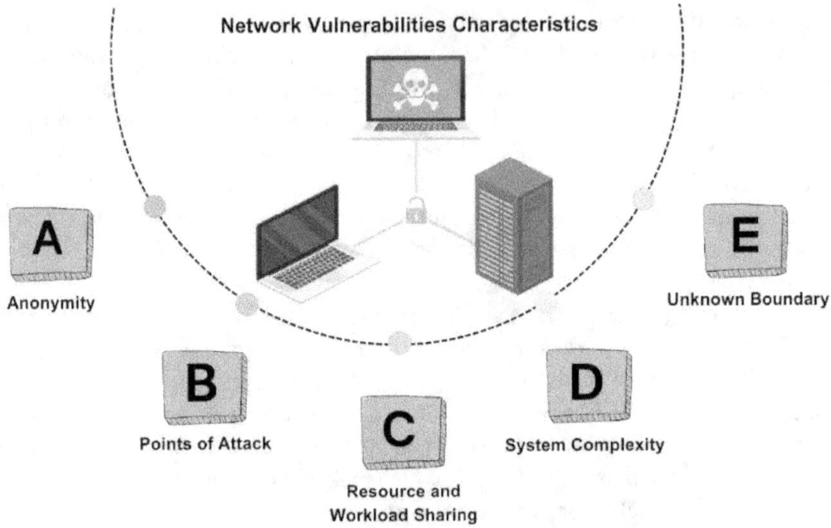

A) **Anonymity:** In a networked environment, an attacker does not need to be physically present with an information system to attack. The attacker could be physically anywhere on the globe and can still mount an attack on a network from outside the network.

B) **Points of attack:** a networked environment can potentially expose many different points of attack. From a security perspective, a network is only as strong as its weakest link, and weak access controls on a single node can expose the entire network to risks.

C) **Resource and Workload sharing:** Although networks allow computational resources and workloads to be shared, this also means more users have access to computational assets, thus exposing those assets to a greater risk.

D) **System Complexity:** computer security expert and columnist Mikko Hyppönen once said complexity is the enemy of security. In big organizations, Network architecture is often complex. Since networks are intrinsically more complex than standalone systems, there is a greater chance that security vulnerability will be overlooked in a networked environment.

E) **Unknown Boundary:** Networks often have unknown boundaries. Since the boundary of a network can change dynamically, it is often difficult to ensure that the entire network is secure. This is especially true in wireless networks, where unknown nodes can join and leave the network on an ad hoc basis.

4.6.1 Network Attacks

A network attack is an attempt to gain unauthorized access to an organization's network, intending to steal data or perform other malicious activity. There are two main types of network attacks:

1. **Passive:** Attackers gain access to a network and can monitor or steal sensitive information without changing the data, leaving it intact.
2. **Active:** Attackers not only gain unauthorized access but also modify data, deleting, encrypting, or otherwise harming it.

A) Types of attacks:

1. **Endpoint Attacks:** Involves gaining unauthorized access to user devices, servers, or other endpoints, typically compromising them by infecting them with malware.
2. **Malware Attacks:** These attacks involve infecting IT resources with malware, allowing attackers to compromise systems, steal data, and cause damage. They also include Ransomware attacks.
3. **Vulnerabilities, Exploits, and Attacks:** Exploiting vulnerabilities in software used in the organization to gain unauthorized access, compromise, or sabotage systems.
4. **Advanced Persistent Threats:** These are complex multilayered threats, which include network attacks but also other attack types.

B) Types of Network Threats:

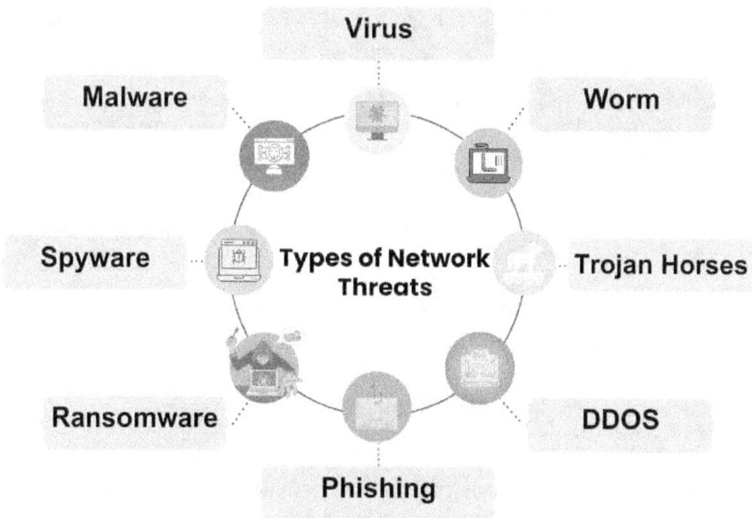

1. **Virus:** A computer virus is like a digital bug, contagious and harmful. It sneaks into your computer by attaching itself to innocent files, just as a bug latches onto a host. Once inside, it can multiply and spread to other files or even to other computers if you share them. Viruses aim to corrupt or erase your files and data. To protect against them, use antivirus software and be cautious about downloading from untrusted sources. Most popular computer virus were Brain (1986), Melissa (1999), ILOVEYOU (2000), Code Red (2001), Conficker (2008).

Domain 4: Network Security

2. **Worm:** Think of a computer worm as a digital traveler, moving between computers over a network like a secret tunnel. It can do this without you doing anything. Worms can copy themselves and potentially harm the systems they infect. To stay safe, keep your software up to date and use a firewall to block unwanted network access. Most popular computer worms were Nimda (2001), Blaster (MSBlast or MSBlaster) (2003), SQL Slammer (2003), Sasser (2004), Mydoom (2004),

3. **Trojan Horse (Trojan):** Imagine a Trojan horse as a tricky gift. It pretends to be harmless but hides something harmful inside. When you open it, the hidden threat emerges, compromising your computer's safety. Trojans often spread via email attachments or disguised as trustworthy software. They can steal your info, give unauthorized access, or turn your computer into part of a network used for bad things. To protect against Trojans, be careful with email attachments and only download from trusted sources.

4. **Distributed Denial-of-Service (DDoS):** Picture a DDoS attack as a massive traffic jam on a website, making it unavailable. Attackers do this by flooding the site with a massive amount of fake traffic, like a protest blocking a store's entrance. DDoS attacks are usually carried out by multiple devices working together. Websites use security measures to filter out this fake traffic and stay online.

5. **Phishing:** Phishing is like a baited hook in a digital sea. Attackers send fake emails or messages that look trustworthy, trying to trick you into revealing personal information like passwords or credit card numbers. They often use a sense of urgency or emotional tricks to get you to click on a link or download something. To stay safe, always check the source of messages and verify website addresses before sharing personal info.

6. **Ransomware:** Ransomware is like digital kidnapping. It locks your files, making them inaccessible, and then demands a ransom for the key to unlock them. To prevent this, regularly back up your data, keep your software updated, and avoid downloading from suspicious sources.

7. **Spyware:** Spyware is like a digital spy hiding in your device. It secretly gathers information about your online activities, such as the websites you visit and your search terms, and then shares this information with unauthorized parties without your knowledge. To protect yourself, use reliable antivirus software, scan your device for spyware, and be cautious about downloading software from unverified sources.

8. **Malware:** Malware is a general term for all sorts of digital threats, including viruses, worms, Trojans, and spyware. Their goal is to harm your computer, steal your data, or otherwise compromise your digital security. Protect yourself by using trustworthy antivirus software, keeping your software updated, and being careful about what you download and click on.

4.6.2 Threat Detection

The battle to protect digital assets and sensitive information hinges on the ability to detect threats before they manifest into full-scale attacks. Threat detection is the ability to identify malicious activity on a network or system. It is an essential part of any cybersecurity strategy, as it can help to prevent security breaches and minimize the damage caused by attacks. While defence mechanisms are crucial, the ability to timely recognize and identify nefarious activities can be the difference between a secure system and a compromised one. By using a combination of threat detection methods, organizations can improve their ability to detect malicious activity early and prevent security breaches. Central to this protective mechanism is the Intrusion Detection System (IDS), a sophisticated tool designed to identify unusual patterns and activities, acting as an early warning system. Early threat detection is essential for any organization that wants to protect itself from cyber threats. By detecting threats early, organizations can prevent security breaches, minimize the damage caused by attacks, improve their security posture, and reduce the cost of security incidents.

A) Intrusion Detection System (IDS):

An Intrusion Detection System (IDS) is a security device that monitors a network or system for malicious activity. IDSes can be used to detect a wide range of threats, including malware, viruses, and unauthorized access attempts. IDSs work by analysing network traffic or system activity for patterns that indicate malicious activity. When an IDS detects suspicious activity, it can generate an alert or take other actions, such as blocking the traffic or system activity. IDSes are an essential part of any cybersecurity strategy. By detecting malicious activity early, IDSes can help prevent security breaches and minimize the damage caused by attacks.

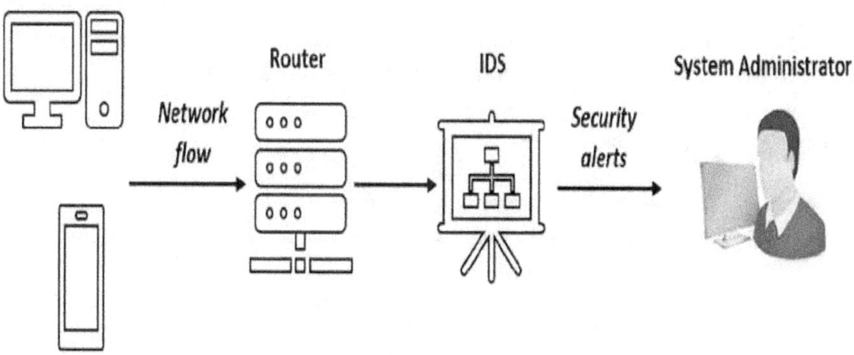

How do intrusion detection systems work?

IDS operates on a fundamental premise: knowing your network so well that it can spot when something unusual or potentially harmful happens. Intrusion

Detection Systems are used to detect anomalies with the aim of catching hackers before they do real damage to a network. IDSes can be either network- or host-based. A host-based intrusion detection system is installed on the client computer, while a network-based intrusion detection system resides on the network.

IDS employs various techniques, including signature-based detection, anomaly-based detection, and heuristics, to identify potential threats. Signature-based detection uses known patterns or signatures of known threats, while anomaly-based detection looks for deviations from normal behaviour. Heuristics, on the other hand, involves analysing behaviour patterns to identify potential threats. Think of it as a surveillance camera, capturing every movement and flagging any suspicious ones.

Critical features of IDS:

- Real-time monitoring and analysis
- Policy-driven detections
- Alarm and alert functions

IDSes come in different flavours and detect suspicious activities using different methods.

B) Host-based Intrusion Detection System (HIDS):

A host-based intrusion detection system (HIDS) is a type of IDS that monitors a single host for malicious activity. HIDSs can be installed on servers, workstations, and other devices, with direct access to both the internet and the enterprise's internal network. HIDSs work by analysing system activity for patterns that indicate malicious activity. This activity can include system calls, file access, and network traffic. A HIDS may also be able to identify malicious traffic that originates from the host itself, such as when the host has been infected with malware and is attempting to spread to other systems. A HIDS has an advantage over a NIDS in that it may be able to detect abnormal network packets that originate from inside the organization or malicious traffic that a NIDS has failed to detect.

Advantages of HIDS:

- Fine-Grained Monitoring: HIDS can offer deep insights into precisely what is happening within a host, right down to the specific processes and system calls.
- Independence: It works even if the network is compromised since it operates at the host level.
- Portable: Ideal for remote devices or ones that frequently switch networks.

C) Network Intrusion Detection System (NIDS)

A network intrusion detection system (NIDS) is a type of IDS that monitors a network for malicious activity. NIDSs work by analyzing network traffic for patterns that indicate malicious activity. This traffic can include incoming and outgoing traffic, as well as traffic between different devices on the network. NIDSs are an essential part of any cybersecurity strategy. By detecting malicious activity early, NIDSs can help prevent security breaches and minimize the damage caused by attacks.

NIDSs can be deployed at strategic points on a network, such as between the network and the internet or between different segments of the network. Based on the placement within a network, NIDS can be categorised into three categories as follows.

1. In-Line NIDS: In-line NIDS is placed directly in the path of network traffic. Every piece of data entering or leaving the network passes through the NIDS sensor. The In-line NIDS devices are strategically placed in the network infrastructure, typically between network segments or at crucial choke points. As traffic flows through these devices, the NIDS continuously analyses packets in real time to detect suspicious patterns or signatures that may indicate an intrusion. The advantage of In-line NIDS is In-line NIDS provides immediate analysis and response, making it effective against fast-moving threats. Some in-line NIDS can actively block malicious traffic as it's detected, acting as a proactive defence mechanism. By inspecting all traffic, in-line NIDS offers a comprehensive view of entire network activities. However, one must keep in mind that as all traffic passes through the NIDS, it can become a potential bottleneck if not correctly scaled to handle network throughput. If the in-line NIDS fails or experiences issues, it can disrupt network traffic, becoming a single point of failure.

2. Out-of-Band NIDS: Out-of-band NIDS operates independently from the primary network traffic flow, like a detective reviewing security footage after an event. Unlike In-line NIDS, this is placed on a separate network segment, usually through a network tap or mirrored port. Instead of analysing traffic in real-time, out-of-band NIDS reviews copies of network packets after they have passed through the network tap. The advantage of this configuration is that Out-of-band NIDS does not directly impact the network's performance, making it less likely to introduce latency or disrupt traffic. Also, it can be easier to scale out-of-band NIDS as it doesn't interfere with the primary network traffic. However, the Out-of-band NIDS may not provide real-time detection and response as it reviews traffic after it has passed through the network. It may miss certain types of attacks that are fleeting or depend on real-time interactions.

3. Network Tap NIDS: Network taps serve as the bridge between network traffic and NIDS sensors, allowing for precise monitoring and analysis. They replicate network traffic, sending a copy to the NIDS for analysis while allowing the original traffic to continue undisturbed. Network Tap NIDS helps overcome the problem of out-of-band NIDs as it provides complete visibility into network traffic without introducing any latency or risk of disruption. It is also used for both in-line and out-of-band deployments, offering flexibility. The Network tap hardware can add to the deployment cost and requires additional hardware to implement and maintain network taps. As a result, they are not as common as the other two NIDS are.

Organizations must carefully assess their network architecture, traffic patterns, and security objectives to determine which NIDS deployment method best aligns with their cybersecurity strategy. Often, a combination of these methods can achieve comprehensive threat detection and network security.

4.6.3 Threat Prevention

Prevention is better than cure because prevention leaves you with certainty that something wrong will not happen. The same is true for cybersecurity as well. As cyber criminals employ increasingly sophisticated techniques, organizations must fortify their defenses to safeguard their digital assets. Cyber threat prevention is the process of taking steps to prevent cyber-attacks from happening in the first place. Early threat prevention is essential for any organization that wants to protect itself from cyber threats. By taking steps to prevent attacks from happening in the first place, organizations can reduce their risk, minimize damage, and improve compliance. A comprehensive cyber threat prevention program includes various technologies. We will look at these technical solutions closely.

A) Intrusion Prevention System (IPS): IPS (Intrusion Prevention System) is like an intelligent security guard for your computer network. It automatically helps stop bad stuff from getting in, making it easier for other security tools to work well. IPS is especially good at finding and stopping hackers who try to use weaknesses in your computer system. Sometimes, these weaknesses are discovered before they can be fixed, and that is when IPS steps in to protect your network. In the past, IPS was a separate machine, but now it is part of more extensive security systems like UTM (Unified Threat Management) and Next-Generation Firewalls. These days, IPS also works with cloud-based services, making it even better at keeping your network safe.

Intrusion Prevention Systems

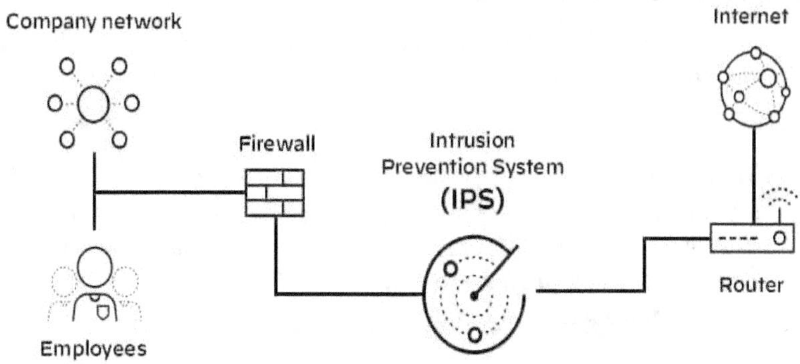

The IPS is mostly placed inline, directly in the flow of network, right behind the perimeter firewall. This is what differentiates IPS from its predecessor, the intrusion detection system (IDS). While IDS is a passive monitoring system that scans traffic and reports back on threats, whereas IPS analyses all data traffic flows that enter the network and takes automated actions when necessary. These actions can include: Sending a notification to the administrator (similar to IDS, Dropping the malicious packets, Blocking traffic from the source address, Resetting the connection, and Configuring firewalls to prevent future attacks. For the IPS to work effectively there are several techniques used by the IPS. These techniques include:

1. **Signature-Based Detection** is a detection method based on a dictionary of uniquely identifiable patterns (or signatures) in the code of each exploit. As an exploit is discovered, its signature is recorded and stored in a continuously growing dictionary of signatures. Signature detection for IPS breaks down into two types:
    - **Exploit-Facing Signatures:** They identify individual exploits by triggering the unique patterns of a particular exploit attempt. The IPS can identify specific exploits by finding a match with an exploit-facing signature in the traffic stream.
    - **Vulnerability-Facing Signatures:** These are broader signatures that target the underlying vulnerability in the system being targeted. These signatures allow networks to be protected from unidentified threats, but they also raise the risk of false positives.
2. **Anomaly-Based Detection** randomly samples network traffic and compares them to a pre-calculated baseline performance level. When the traffic activity is outside the parameters of baseline performance, the IPS takes action.
3. **Policy-Based Detection** requires system administrators to configure security policies based on an organization's security policies and network

infrastructure. If any activity occurs that breaks a defined security policy, an alert is triggered and sent to the admins.

B) Types of Intrusion Prevention Systems:

1. **Network-Based Intrusion Prevention System (NIPS):** It is installed at strategic points to monitor all network traffic and scan for threats.
2. **Host Intrusion Prevention System (HIPS):** This system is installed on an endpoint and looks at inbound and outbound traffic from that machine only. Often combined with NIPS, it serves as a last line of defence against threats.
3. **Network Behavior Analysis (NBA):** It analyzes network traffic to detect unusual traffic flows and spot new malware or zero-day vulnerabilities.
4. **Wireless intrusion prevention system (WIPS):** It scans a Wi-Fi network for unauthorized access and removes any unauthorized devices.

4.7 Firewalls

The Internet is a Public Network. Being a public network used by people with good intentions and bad intentions. To protect computers from people with bad intentions a firewall is used. When surfing the internet many dangers in the form of malware are trying to harm computers. Hackers are all trying to gain access to every computer connected to the Internet. Just like a security fence around a building protects a home from burglars and intruders, a firewall keeps Cyber criminals and hackers from penetrating a private network. A firewall's purpose is to create a safety barrier between a private network and the public internet. A firewall acts as a defense system for a network against viruses, worms, Trojans, brute force attacks, and other network attacks or attacks that attempts to compromise a network. Firewalls can take the form of software, such as a security program, or hardware, such as a physical router. Both perform the same function, which is scanning incoming network traffic to make sure it doesn't contain blacklisted data. The firewall scans each packet of data, which are small chunks of the larger hole reduced in size for easy transmission, and makes sure these packets don't contain anything malicious. Internet security software companies often bundle firewall solutions built into their antivirus programs.

4.7.1 Generations of Firewall

A) First Generation: In 1988, engineers from Digital Equipment Corporation developed the first and simple generation of firewalls known as packet filter firewalls. This firewall is used to inspect packets transferred between computers. The firewall maintained an access control list that dictates what packets will be looked at and what action should be applied. The default action is set to discard the packet silently. Three essential actions regarding the packet consist of a silent discard, discard with Internet Control Message Protocol or TCP reset response to the sender, and forward to the next hop. Packets were filtered by source and destination IP addresses protocol, and source and destination ports. The bulk of Internet communication in the 20th and early 21st century used either Transmission Control Protocol (TCP) or User Datagram Protocol (UDP) in conjunction with well-known ports, enabling firewalls of that era to distinguish between specific types of traffic such as web browsing, remote printing, email transmission, file transfer.

B) Second Generation: The second-generation firewall introduced the concept of a connection state. From the perspective of a firewall, when users are on a network, there are two zones. Trusted zone and an untrusted zone. So, the trusted zone is permitted to go to the untrusted zone, but the untrusted zone is not permitted to go to the trusted zone unless specified in the configuration. When a user on a LAN is browsing the web, the user goes out to a web server over the Internet, and then the user has to open a connection to allow that return traffic to come back. When that connection is no longer needed, the firewall breaks the connection down. This generation of firewalls attempted to increase the level of security between trusted and untrusted networks. Known as application proxy or gateway firewalls, this approach to protection is significantly different from packet filters and Stateful packet inspection. An application gateway firewall uses software to intercept connections for each Internet protocol and to perform security inspections. It involves what is commonly known as proxy services. These circuit-level firewalls are simply an upgraded version of the first generation. They were required to keep up with advancing computer-to-computer linking technology through the internet.

C) Third generation: This generation firewall introduced application visibility, an application-level filter. It was state-of-the-art perimeter security integrated within major network components. These systems alert administrators in real time about suspicious activity that may be occurring on their systems. This generation of firewalls has evolved to meet the significant requirements demanded by corporate networks of increased security while minimizing the impact on network performance. The requirements of the third generation of firewalls were more demanding due to the growing support for VPNs, wireless communication, and enhanced virus protection. These new firewalls understood how many protocols typically work. It knew how FTP worked, it knew how email and SMTP worked, and if some rogue application tried to hijack one of those ports and protocols and make it behave in a way that it was not supposed to, the application filter used to shut down the connection. The most challenging element of this evolution was maintaining the firewall's simplicity without compromising flexibility and Security.

D) Next Generation: A next-generation firewall (NGFW) is, as Gartner defines it, a "deep-packet inspection firewall that moves beyond port/protocol inspection and blocking to add application-level inspection, intrusion prevention, and bringing intelligence from outside the firewall." Next-generation firewalls are a more advanced version of the traditional firewall, and they offer the same benefits. Like regular firewalls, NGFW uses both static and dynamic packet filtering and VPN support to ensure that all connections between the network, internet, and firewall are valid and secure. These firewalls have extensive control and visibility of applications that can identify malicious traffic/packets using analysis and signature matching. They can use whitelists or a signature-based IPS to distinguish between safe applications and unwanted ones, which are then identified using SSL decryption. Unlike most traditional firewalls, NGFWs also include a path through which future updates will be received.

4.7.2 Hardware vs Software Firewalls

A) Hardware Firewalls: A hardware firewall sits between an organization's local network of computers and the Internet. The firewall usually inspects all the data that comes in from the Internet, passing along the safe data packets while blocking the potentially dangerous packets. To adequately protect a network without hindering performance, hardware firewalls require expert setup, so Hardware Firewalls may not be a feasible solution for companies without a dedicated IT department. For businesses with many computers, however, being able to control network security from one single device simplifies the job.

B) Software Firewalls: Software firewalls are installed on individual computers on a network. Unlike hardware firewalls, software firewalls can easily distinguish between programs on a computer. This lets them allow data to one program while blocking another. Software firewalls can also filter outgoing data and remote responses to outgoing requests. The major downside to software firewalls for a business is their upkeep: They require installation, updating, and administration on each computer.

C) Hybrid Firewall: To share an Internet connection between multiple computers, routers must distinguish which pieces of data need to go to which computer. The process of separating the data acts as a kind of firewall. If unwanted data comes in, the router will not identify it as belonging to any computer and thus will discard it. This level of protection serves adequately for home use, along with a software firewall. It's also enough for many business networks that don't require high security. However, routers generally lack the options and advanced features that dedicated hardware firewalls offer. Using a single software firewall along with a router or hardware firewall will strengthen network security without losing any compatibility issues. Using multiple software firewalls, however, can cause conflicts, hampering proper operation. Businesses highly concerned with network security can put together multiple hardware firewalls, minimizing any weaknesses in each. However, this requires careful expert setup to avoid incompatibilities and blocking of legitimate data traffic.

Firewalls, both hardware and software, protect computers from hackers and other online threats by blocking dangerous pieces of data from reaching the system. While hardware firewalls offer network-wide protection from external threats, software firewalls installed on individual computers can more closely inspect data, and can block specific programs from even sending data to the Internet. On networks with high security concerns, combining both kinds of firewalls provides a complete safety net.

D) Types of Firewalls:

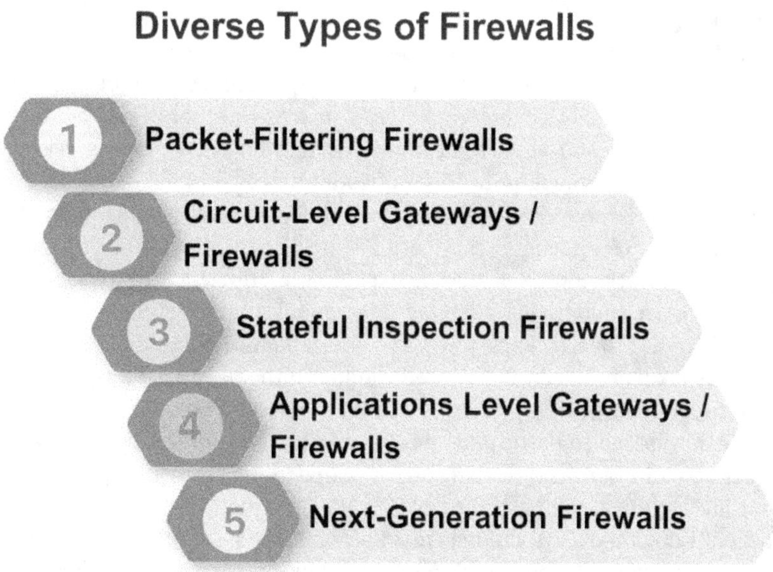

1) Packet Filters: A packet-filtering firewall examines each packet that crosses the firewall and tests the packet according to a set of rules set up during initial configuration. If the packet passes the test, it's allowed to enter the network. If the packet doesn't pass, it's rejected or discarded. Packet filters are the least expensive type of firewall. As a result, packet-filtering firewalls are very common. However, packet filtering has some flaws that knowledgeable hackers can exploit. As a result, packet filtering by itself doesn't make for a fully effective firewall. Packet filters work by inspecting the source and destination IP and port addresses contained in each Transmission Control Protocol/Internet Protocol (TCP/IP) packet. TCP/IP ports are numbers that are assigned to specific services that help to identify for which service each packet is intended. For example, the port number for the HTTP protocol is 80. As a result, any incoming packets headed for an HTTP server will specify port 80 as the destination port.

Port numbers are often specified with a colon following an IP address. For example, the HTTP service on a server whose IP address is 192.168.10.133 would be 192.168.10.133:80. The rules that administrators set up for the packet filter either permit or deny packets that specify specific IP addresses or ports. For example, administrators may permit packets that are intended for mail servers or web servers and deny all other packets.

2) Circuit-Level Gateways / Firewalls: A circuit-level gateway monitors TCP handshaking between packets from trusted clients or servers to untrusted hosts and vice versa to determine whether a requested session is legitimate. To filter packets in this way, a circuit-level gateway relies on data contained in the packet headers for the Internet's TCP session-layer protocol. Because a circuit-level gateway filters packets at the session layer of the OSI model, this gateway operates two layers higher than a packet-filtering firewall does. Monitoring Handshaking--Circuitously. To determine whether a requested session is legitimate, a circuit-level gateway uses a process similar to the following: A trusted client requests a service, and the gateway accepts this request, assuming that the client meets basic filtering criteria (such as whether DNS can locate the client's IP address and associated name). Acting on behalf of the client, the gateway opens a connection to the requested untrusted host and then closely monitors the TCP handshaking that follows. This handshaking involves an exchange of TCP packets that are flagged SYN (synchronize) or ACK (acknowledge). These packet types are legitimate only at specific points during the session. A circuit-level gateway determines that a requested session is legitimate only if the SYN flags, ACK flags, and sequence numbers involved in the TCP handshaking between the trusted client and the untrusted host are logical. After a circuit-level gateway determines that the trusted client and the untrusted host are authorized to participate in a TCP session and verifies the legitimacy of this session, the gateway establishes a connection. From this point on, the circuit-level gateway simply copies and forwards packets back and forth without further filtering them. The gateway maintains a table of established connections, allowing data to pass when session information matches an entry in the table. When the session is completed, the gateway removes the associated entry in the table and closes the circuit this session used.

3) Stateful Inspection Firewalls: A stateful firewall is nothing but a combination of Packet Filters and a Circuit-level gateway. This type of Firewall inspects both the packets and handshake. Any traffic that does not fit the pre-configured criteria will drop the connection. This firewall monitors the entire state of active network connections. This means that stateful firewalls are constantly analyzing the complete context of traffic and data packets, seeking entry to a network rather than discrete traffic and data packets in isolation. Once a stateful firewall has approved a certain kind of traffic, it is added to a state table and can travel more freely into the protected network. Traffic and data packets that don't complete the required handshake will be blocked. By considering multiple factors before adding a type of connection to an approved list, such as TCP stages, stateful firewalls can observe traffic streams in their entirety.

4) Applications Level Gateways / Firewalls: Commonly known as the proxy firewall, this firewall operates at the Application layer by combining the attributes of both packet-filtering firewalls and circuit-level gateways. This firewall first establishes a connection to the source of the traffic and scans through the application layer when inspecting the incoming data packet. The verification is much more thorough on this firewall as it verifies the TCP handshake protocol as well as the contents of the packets. Another advantage of this firewall is that it has its IP address, hence can prevent direct contact with any other networks. Firewalls working at the application level provide additional anonymity & data security and have advanced logging & inspection abilities. Still, they adversely affect the network performance due to the extra steps in the data packet verification process.

Application-specific proxies accept only packets generated by services they are designed to copy, forward and filter. For example, only a Telnet proxy can copy, forward, and filter Telnet traffic. If a network relies only on an application-level gateway, incoming and outgoing packets cannot access services for which there is no proxy. Unlike a circuit-level gateway, an application-level gateway runs proxies that examine and filter individual packets rather than simply copying them and blindly forwarding them across the gateway. Application-specific proxies check each packet that passes through the gateway, verifying the contents of the packet up through the application layer (which is the highest layer) of the OSI model. These proxies can filter particular kinds of commands or information in the application protocols; the proxies are designed to copy, forward, and filter.

5) Next-Generation Firewall: The reality is that the firewall is rapidly evolving, not only in what it can do but also in its business value to the enterprise. It is becoming the cornerstone of hybrid cloud network security, offering integration enablement, consistent controls, and comprehensive monitoring and alerting across multiple cloud and on-premises environments. Simultaneously, the firewall's feature set is expanding beyond the realm of traditional network security to include a fascinating variety of features not necessarily limited to security. Looking forward, key technological developments, including encryption, artificial intelligence/machine learning (AI/ML), and the Internet of Things (IoT), will arguably make the enterprise firewall more critical than it has ever been. A next-generation firewall seeks to improve network security by inspecting more layers of the OSI model and looking at the contents of the data packets to make filtering decisions. In essence, a next-generation firewall consolidates various established security mechanisms into a single device, intending to make the security more accessible to manage and so make it more effective.

The next-generation firewall is expected to include the following technologies.

- TLS/SSL decryption to spot data exfiltration
- Web content filtering
- Monitor or block the use of cloud-sharing platforms and redirect users to approved solutions.
- Intrusion Detection and Intrusion Prevention

- Malware scanning and detection

4.8 Antivirus

Antivirus software, also referred to as AV Software, is a class of programs designed to protect, prevent, detect, and remove malware infections on computing devices, networks, and IT systems. Antivirus software, originally designed to detect and remove malware from computers, can also protect against a wide variety of threats, including other types of malicious software, such as key-loggers, browser hijackers, Trojan horses, worms, rootkits, spyware, adware, botnets, and Ransomware, etc. The early versions of Anti-virus programs were signature-based identification mechanisms. As the nature of the malware changed over time, similarly the Antivirus programs evolved and included various components to deal with the ever-growing and evolving threats and malware.

How Anti-Virus works: When an antivirus program is installed, it will start monitoring the activity of the system by searching files that are being created, Accessed, modified, Transferred, and stored to or from the hard disks and external/removable drives. Files that are being downloaded from the Internet are also scanned. If suspicious activity is detected, the antivirus program will automatically quarantine the file or stop the processes that are posing a risk to the operating system, contacts, or other computers or devices in the network unless the user trusts the file and allows it to continue its work.

Traditional detection-based antivirus products have had a firm hold on the security market for years. However, recently, due to an exponential rise in Cybercrime and malware, these traditional antiviruses have been rendered ineffective against many emerging threats. All the executable programs that pass through the system go through an antivirus scan. They then undergo a comparison test with the blacklisted signatures. If they appear to be the same as a blacklisted one, then they are considered to be a malware file. The other program files are then processed through Defense + HIPS (Host Intrusion Prevention System) – this permits only the known files. In contrast, the unknown files that look suspicious are moved into a restricted virtual environment. The identified suitable files are documented in the Whitelist, while the suspicious files will be quarantined in the Sandboxed environment.

4.8.1 Scan Engines

The Scan Engine is the core of the Antivirus Program. Antivirus applications use two types of scanner engines: on-demand scanners that are activated only by the user to scan a part or all of the computer, and on-access (otherwise called real-time, background guard, resident shield, and auto-protect) scanners that monitor data in real-time, i.e., while data is coming into a computer, files are being opened, and during similar actions.

Almost all Anti-virus programs offer various scans. The most common types are.

A) Full Scan: As the name suggests, this scan checks everything present in the system. This can usually take a few hours to complete if the system happens to have a lot of data stored on it. The Antivirus system usually scans the following when it is running a full scan of the system:

1. All network drives, hard drives, and removable storage.
2. System memory (RAM).
3. System Backups.
4. Start-up folders.
5. Registry items.

Most AV vendors recommend a complete system scan every two weeks.

B) Quick Scan: A quick scan (or its equivalent) targets the entire system, but it does not take as much time as a full scan; the files that they scan are the following:

1. Commonly infected files and folders.
2. Running processes and threads.
3. System memory (RAM).
4. Startup folders.
5. Registry items.

This may seem quite similar to the files that are scanned during a full scan, but what sets it apart is that this system analyzes the most likely folders instead of every single one. It also focuses only on the files that have been modified since the last scan.

C) Real-Time / On-Access Scan: This is a persistent and ongoing scan. Each time a file is received, opened, downloaded, copied, or modified, Real-time Scan scans the file for security risks. If a real-time scan detects no security risk, the file remains in its location, and users can proceed to access the file. If a real-time scan detects a security risk, it takes action set in the policy (e.g. quarantine/ block / delete, etc). It displays a notification message, showing the name of the infected file, the specific security risk, and the action taken on the threat. This Scan actively monitors the system memory and all the typical virus and security risk locations on the computer quickly. The scan includes all processes that run in memory, important registry files, and files such as config.sys and windows.ini. It also includes some critical operating system folders.

4.8.2 Multi-Role Antivirus

Traditional Antivirus software only had signature-based scans. As the nature of malware and cyber-attacks has changed over time, Antivirus software has also evolved to mitigate the ever-changing nature of these attacks. Several new features have been added to Antivirus software. Let us have a look at them.

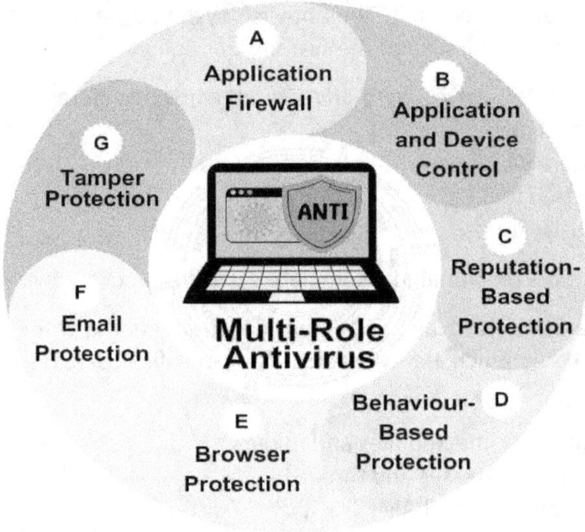

A) Application Firewall: The AV also contains an application-based Firewall. This component monitors all active network connections on the endpoint and all incoming and outgoing traffic for suspicious activity. It also includes the Intrusion Prevention component.

B) Application and Device Control: This feature allows the cybersecurity engineer to control which applications are allowed to be installed and used on the machine. Applications can be blocked based on their signature or class. The same is valid for devices. Specific devices can be allowed, while others (such as removable drives) can be blocked.

C) Reputation-Based Protection: Signature-based scans have limitations. The AV cannot hold the signatures of all applications. This is when the Antivirus can connect to the central cloud-based database to check the reputation of a file or program. Based on the reputation, the application is either allowed or blocked.

D) Behaviour-Based Protection: Heuristic scanning is a technique used to catch malicious applications. While traditional signature-based systems rely on predefined virus signatures to catch viruses, heuristics looks at the construction of files for characteristics commonly found in viruses. As a file is examined, the virus-like attributes are totalled. If a threshold in the number of virus-like attributes is passed, the file is marked as 'suspicious.'

E) Browser Protection: This feature monitors the activity of the Browsers installed on the computer. It helps protect a computer from drive-by infection and scans files being downloaded using a browser. It also warns and protects against malicious websites. This feature may also block BHO (Browser Helper Objects) from installing or monitoring user activity.

F) Email Protection: This feature monitors Outlook or similar mail client programs' mailboxes. Every incoming and outgoing email is scanned, and malicious emails are deleted or quarantined. This feature is handy for protecting against emails sent to a target user's PC with Ransomware.

G) Tamper Protection: A retrovirus is also referred to as an anti-anti-virus virus. This type of malware tries to attack and disable any anti-virus or protective software on the system and is trying to infect to avoid detection. These viruses try to disable/deactivate the Antivirus software by stopping changing or lowering security settings, Registry changes, or group policies. The Tamper protection feature monitors all these features to ensure that malware is not able to disable or lower the security of the computer.

4.9 Understand Network Security Infrastructure

In our modern digital era, the security of our online world has taken center stage. Imagine the internet as a vast, interconnected realm, much like a bustling city. In this chapter, we'll explore network security infrastructure in terms that are easy to understand and free from technical jargon, giving you the tools to grasp its importance.

A) The Foundation of Digital Security

Visualize the internet as a thriving city with your digital devices as towering buildings within this virtual landscape. Network security infrastructure can be compared to the bedrock, a foundational yet often overlooked part that provides stability and protection.

B) The Building Blocks: Hardware and Software

Network security infrastructure consists of two key components: hardware and software. Hardware includes physical devices such as routers and switches, while software encompasses applications and configurations that act as guardians to protect your data. Together, they form an impenetrable shield, securing your digital city.

C) Safeguarding Data: Encryption

When you send data online, it is like mailing a letter through the city's postal system. Encryption plays a crucial role in ensuring the safety of this information. It's akin to placing your letter in a securely locked box before sending it, ensuring that even if someone intercepts it, they can't decipher its contents without the correct key.

D) Digital Traffic Regulations

Just as a city has traffic rules to maintain order, network security infrastructure has its own set of "rules" governing how data should be handled.

E) Access Control

Think of access control as establishing rules for who can enter a building. Network security infrastructure sets the boundaries for accessing specific information, ensuring that only authorized individuals can enter certain segments of your digital city.

F) Intrusion Detection

Imagine surveillance cameras keeping an eye on a city to identify unusual activities. Intrusion detection performs a similar function within your digital world. It vigilantly watches over network traffic, promptly alerting you to any suspicious actions, much like a city's security team keeping an eye on events for any anomalies.

G) Preventing Digital Congestion

Network security infrastructure ensures the uninterrupted flow of data within your digital city, similar to how a city manages traffic.

H) Load Balancing

Think of load balancing as traffic signals that redirect cars to less congested routes during a traffic jam. In your digital city, it ensures an even distribution of data traffic, preventing overloads on specific pathways and maintaining a smooth flow of information.

I) Redundancy

Just as a city has multiple power sources to prevent blackouts, network security infrastructure includes redundancy. It establishes backups and alternatives to ensure that if one segment of your digital city encounters an issue, your data remains accessible and secure.

J) Monitoring and Reporting

Network security infrastructure is not just a foundation; it also acts as a watchful guardian.

K) Security Information and Event Management (SIEM)

SIEM serves as a digital command center that continuously monitors and reports on the activities within your digital city. It collects data from various sources, conducts analysis, and provides insights to help identify and respond to potential security threats.

L) Your Role in the Digital City

As a resident of your digital city, you play a vital role in upholding security.

1. **Awareness:** Stay informed about common online threats and best practices for safe digital living. Just as you are aware of safety guidelines in your city, your digital city requires a similar level of vigilance.
2. **Protection:** Utilize strong and unique passwords to secure your devices and online accounts. Think of them as the keys to your digital home.
3. **Data Responsibility:** Just as you exercise caution when sharing sensitive information with strangers in your city, apply the same level of care when sharing personal details online.

4.9.1 Understanding On-Premises Essentials

In our modern age of technology, terms like "the cloud" and "data centers" often take the spotlight. However, there is a crucial element that hums quietly in the background—the on-premises infrastructure. In this chapter, we will examine these essential components more closely, and we promise there won't be any technical jargon to confuse you, regardless of your tech-savvyness.

A) The Solid Ground Beneath You

Imagine your digital world as a bustling city filled with digital devices and services. Now, picture the on-premises infrastructure as the bedrock that this city stands upon. This vital foundation includes various components like power, data centers or closets, Heating, Ventilation, and Air Conditioning (HVAC), environmental controls, fire suppression systems, redundancy, and a few agreements that keep everything running like clockwork.

B) Power - The Lifeblood

Power is like the electricity that keeps your home illuminated. In this digital city, power ensures that all your devices, servers, and network equipment have the energy they need to keep on trucking. Just like a power outage at home can disrupt your daily routine, a loss of power in the digital realm can bring your digital world to a standstill.

C) Data Centers/Closets - Digital Warehouses

Think of data centers and closets as ultra-secure, digital warehouses for your valuable data and applications. They're like those safety deposit boxes in a bank where you keep your most treasured possessions. These facilities are the guardians of your servers, networking equipment, and data, making sure they're both safe and easily accessible.

D) HVAC - Digital Climate Control

Domain 4: Network Security

Heating, Ventilation, and Air Conditioning (HVAC) systems act as the digital climate control for your city, just like your thermostat at home. These systems maintain the right temperature and humidity levels, preventing equipment from overheating and ensuring that everything runs smoothly, even when the weather gets a bit extreme.

E) Environmental Controls - Fine-Tuning

Environmental controls play the role of digital meteorologists in your city. They monitor conditions like temperature and humidity, making sure that the environment is just right for your equipment to work at its best. Much like how you adjust your home's thermostat for comfort, these controls fine-tune the digital city's conditions for peak performance.

F) Fire Suppression - Digital Firefighters

Fire suppression systems are like the brave firefighters of your digital city, always ready to leap into action in case of a fire. They ensure that a blaze is swiftly contained and extinguished, preventing any harm to your equipment.

G) Redundancy - Backup Plans

Redundancy serves as a safety net for unforeseen situations. In the digital world, it ensures that if one piece of equipment or system fails, there's a backup ready to step in. This redundancy is much like having spare tyres in your car – ensuring that even if you encounter a flat, you can continue your journey without a hitch.

H) MOU/MOA - Agreements for Cooperation

Memorandum of Understanding (MOU) and Memorandum of Agreement (MOA) are similar to the rules and agreements that keep your physical neighborhood running smoothly. These documents outline the responsibilities and expectations of different parties in your digital city. They promote cooperation and ensure that everyone works together effectively, understanding their roles in maintaining the digital community's functionality.

I) Your Role in the Digital City

Even if you're not a tech wizard, your role is vital to keeping things ticking smoothly in your digital city.

1. **Energy Awareness:** Just as you are mindful of turning off lights at home when they're not needed, consider the energy efficiency of your digital devices. Reducing energy consumption not only conserves resources but also extends the life of your digital city's infrastructure.
2. **Data Management:** Think of your data as the cherished possessions in your home. Use it prudently and ensure it is well-protected. Please back up your data regularly and follow security best practices to keep it safe from potential threats.

3. **Adherence to Agreements:** Similar to understanding and following community guidelines in your physical neighbourhood, it's essential to abide by any MOUs or MOAs that apply to your digital city. Cooperation and compliance ensure that your digital world operates harmoniously.

4.9.2 Securing Your Digital World

As we continue our journey through the domain of digital security, we arrive at a crucial juncture where we uncover the bedrock strategies that establish a sturdy defense system for your digital realm. Picture your digital domain as a grand castle, and these strategies serve as the ingenious fortifications that shield it from unwelcome intruders. In this chapter, we will delve into these pivotal strategies in plain, understandable language, ensuring that everyone, regardless of their technical background, can grasp their significance.

A) Network Segmentation:

Think of network segmentation as the method used to construct robust walls around your digital castle. These walls create distinct zones within your network, ensuring that if one area is compromised, the others remain secure.

Domain 4: Network Security

1. **Demilitarized Zone (DMZ):** Imagine the DMZ as the drawbridge and the outer courtyard of your castle. It's a partially open space where your public-facing services, such as your website, are located. This buffer area separates them from your more sensitive internal regions.
2. **Virtual Local Area Network (VLAN):** VLANs are like the invisible, protective barriers within your castle. They divide your network into smaller, isolated zones, each with its own set of rules. This ensures that data flows securely within each zone, preventing unauthorized access.
3. **Virtual Private Network (VPN):** Picture VPNs as secret tunnels connecting different parts of your digital kingdom. They provide secure passages for data to travel between remote locations. Only authorized users with the correct key can enter these tunnels.
4. **Micro-segmentation:** Micro-segmentation is akin to having invisible walls within your castle, separating each room. Each room possesses its protection, making it incredibly challenging for an intruder to navigate.

B) Defense in Depth:

The concept of defense in depth is similar to constructing multiple layers of security. Visualize your castle fortified not with a single moat and wall but with several layers, so that if someone breaches one, they encounter another. Defense in depth helps protect systems by providing redundancy, reducing the risk of a single point of failure.

1. **Firewalls:** These serve as the mystical barriers surrounding your castle. They examine all incoming and outgoing traffic, allowing only authorized data to pass through.
2. **Antivirus Software:** Antivirus software functions as your vigilant guard. They continuously patrol your digital castle, searching for any suspicious characters attempting to infiltrate. They stand as your first line of defense against viruses and malware.
3. **Intrusion Detection Systems (IDS):** IDS are like watchful sentinels patrolling your digital domain. They keep a vigilant eye on network traffic and are ready to raise the alarm if they detect any suspicious activity.

C) Network Access Control (NAC):

Think of Network Access Control as the guardian of the gateway to your castle, ensuring that only authorized guests can enter. This is crucial for both your primary network and devices like embedded systems and Internet of Things (IoT) gadgets.

1. **Segmentation for Embedded Systems:** Embedded systems can be compared to the concealed chambers within your castle, each serving a specific role. NAC ensures they remain isolated from the leading network, reducing the risk of compromise.

2. **Internet of Things (IoT):** IoT devices resemble the enchanted objects within your castle. NAC ensures that they have limited access, preventing them from unintentionally aiding potential attackers.
3. **Cloud Ecosystems:** Exploring Service-Level Agreements, Managed Service Providers, SaaS, IaaS, PaaS, and Hybrid Deployments

In our digital journey, we have encountered the term "the cloud," something you might have heard but not fully grasped. Don't worry; we're here to shed light on it and explore its various aspects in plain language, making it accessible to everyone, regardless of their technical background.

D) Cloud Services:

Think of the cloud as a helpful digital service for your computer, like a trusty friend. It's not an actual cloud in the sky; instead, it's a network of powerful computers and servers located in data centers worldwide. These digital pals store, process, and manage data and applications. They offer services that can benefit both individuals and businesses.

The cloud is like a virtual assistant that can take care of tasks for you. It can store your photos, host your website, or run complex software applications. These powerful computers are designed to be accessible from anywhere with an internet connection. It's like having a dependable friend who's always there to lend a hand, no matter where you are.

E) Service-Level Agreement (SLA):

When you and your digital friend, the cloud service provider, team up, you agree to specific terms, similar to a contract. This agreement, known as a Service-Level Agreement (SLA), outlines what the provider will do for you, including the level of service, support, and performance you can expect. It's like setting the rules of engagement between you and your digital friend.

Think of the SLA as a digital handshake, a friendly agreement between you and the cloud provider. Just as you have expectations in your relationships with friends, this agreement sets clear expectations about how your digital friend will assist you. It ensures you receive the level of service and support you need.

F) Managed Service Provider (MSP):

Imagine a Managed Service Provider (MSP) as a reliable butler for your digital needs. MSPs offer various services, including managing your cloud infrastructure, ensuring everything runs smoothly, and providing technical support. They handle the technical details, letting you focus on your tasks, just like a butler keeps your home in order.

In the realm of digital services, MSPs are like personal concierges. They deal with the complexities of managing your cloud resources, making sure they are secure, well-maintained, and always available. Just as a butler ensures that your home runs smoothly, MSPs ensure your digital space is in tip-top shape.

G) Software as a Service (SaaS): Apps in the Cloud

Software as a Service (SaaS) is like accessing your favorite apps or software over the internet. Instead of installing these on your computer, you use them directly from the cloud. It's similar to using a web-based email service like Gmail instead of a desktop email client. You access SaaS applications through a web browser, making them available from anywhere with an internet connection.

Picture SaaS as a collection of digital tools at your fingertips. You don't need to install or update software on your computer; you can use these applications instantly through your web browser. It's like having a suite of apps that you can use on any device, whether it's your home computer, work laptop, or even your smartphone. It's all made possible by your digital friend, the cloud.

H) Infrastructure as a Service (IaaS):

Imagine Infrastructure as a Service (IaaS) as your virtual computer in the cloud. It provides you with the building blocks for your digital world. With IaaS, you can rent virtual machines, storage, and networks on the cloud, just like renting an office space, instead of building your own from scratch. It's cost-effective and flexible, allowing you to scale up or down as needed.

IaaS is like having a digital toolbox. You don't need to worry about buying and maintaining physical hardware; instead, you can rent virtual machines and storage as you need them. It's like renting an office space that you can customize without the hassles of property management. The cloud offers you a virtual playground to build your digital world.

I) Platform as a Service (PaaS): Building Blocks for Developers

For developers, a Platform-as-a-Service (PaaS) is like a digital playground. It provides the tools and environment for developers to build, test, and deploy applications without worrying about the underlying infrastructure. It's like having a well-equipped workshop where you can focus on creating without being bogged down by technical details.

PaaS is the developer's best friend. It offers a set of tools and services that simplify the process of creating and launching applications. Just as an artist needs a studio to work on their masterpieces, developers need a digital environment to bring their creations to life. PaaS provides the canvas and brushes for their digital art.

J) Hybrid Cloud:

Think of a Hybrid Cloud as having the best of both digital and physical worlds. It's like combining your local workshop with your digital playground. In a hybrid cloud setup, you use both on-premises infrastructure and cloud services together. This allows you to leverage the benefits of the cloud while still keeping some of your resources on your local servers, maintaining control and security.

A hybrid cloud is like having a two-sided workspace. You have your physical office where you keep sensitive documents and your local workshop where you work on special projects. At the same time, you have your digital playground in the cloud, giving you access to vast resources and tools. It's all about finding the right balance between physical and digital spaces.

The cloud is not just a technology trend; it's your digital ally. It empowers individuals and businesses to access powerful resources, software, and services without the need for extensive technical knowledge. With a clear understanding of these cloud concepts, you're well on your way to making the most of this valuable digital friend. Just as you rely on a trustworthy friend for support, the cloud is here to simplify your digital life and enhance your capabilities. Embrace it, and let it be your ally in the digital world.

Domain 5: Security Operations

In today's complex digital landscape, the fusion of IT security and IT operations—commonly referred to as SecOps—has become pivotal. This integration ensures that security measures do not restrain IT performance, even as security threats evolve and present new challenges. Originating from the success of the DevOps methodology, which resolved misalignments between development and operations teams, SecOps extends this philosophy to include security, aiming for a seamless operational flow throughout the IT infrastructure.

Security Operations

The Genesis of SecOps

DevOps's achievements did not just inspire the concept of SecOps but is a natural evolution of them. DevOps, a methodology that harmonizes the objectives of Development (Dev) and IT Operations (Ops), has revolutionized software development across various industries. Given these advancements, the progression into merging security with operations was a natural evolution. The primary goal of SecOps is to align IT security and operations teams, ensuring that all processes, particularly those involving DevOps, are conducted securely and efficiently.

This section discusses the core activities that ensure our operational security, exploring the essentials of Configuration, Patch, and Change Management. We also examine critical areas such as Cryptography, Hashing, and the various Attacks that target our Encryption systems.

Further, we explore the complexities of Data Storage, Handling, and Retention, critical components that manage and protect our information assets over time.

Administrative Controls also play a pivotal role in this domain, where we address the importance of Training and Awareness programs and the impacts of Social Engineering.

As we explore this chapter in detail, we will uncover the practical measures and strategies that safeguard our daily operations and fortify our defenses against potential security breaches.

5.1 Configuration Management

Configuration management is a vital preventative control within our cybersecurity framework, ensuring that our environments remain secure through proactive measures. When deploying a new system, whether purchased or developed, it often begins in an inherently vulnerable state: ports are open, and systems may be unpatched. This default openness requires a strict and consistent approach to securing the system. In cloud environments, effective configuration management includes automated configuration tools, regular compliance checks, and version control to ensure consistent security policies across all instances. Proper management helps prevent misconfigurations that could lead to security breaches and supports rapid recovery in case of incidents.

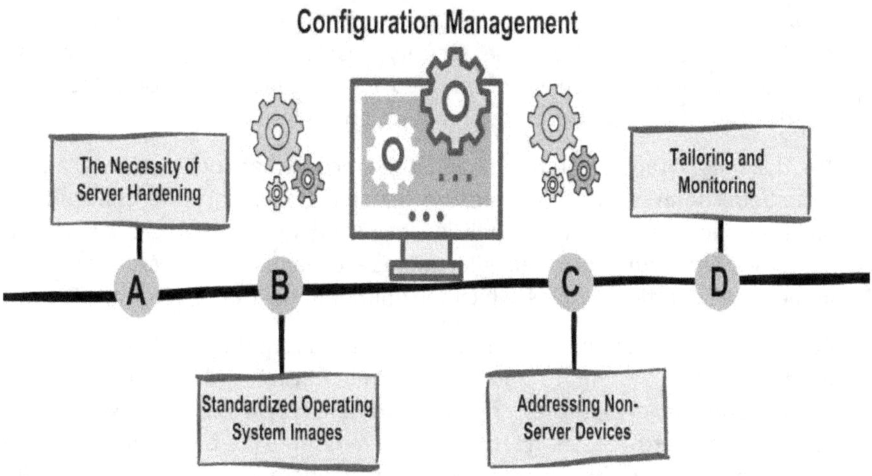

A) The Necessity of Server Hardening

In practice, secure defaults are the exception rather than the rule. Thus, securing a system involves a comprehensive checklist—closing unnecessary ports, disabling or deleting unneeded accounts and services, and applying all critical patches. This process, known as server hardening, is something we have touched on previously.

Each organization typically has a server hardening protocol. However, such standardized processes may not exist for other devices like networking devices or wireless access points. These devices often rely on less formal, ad-hoc lists maintained by responsible teams, such as the networking group. With a strict and formal process, vulnerabilities may remain due to complete security practices.

B) Standardized Operating System Images

Many organizations employ a hardened operating system image to enhance security and efficiency. This standardized image is updated with new patches as vulnerabilities are discovered and then deployed to new servers, avoiding the need for repetitive system installations and manual hardening.

C) Addressing Non-Server Devices

While servers often receive adequate attention, other critical components like switches, routers, workstations, and wireless access points may not. Configuration management should encompass these devices under the principle of least privilege—granting them only the permissions necessary for functionality.

D) Tailoring and Monitoring

Configuration management does not stop at deployment. Continuously monitoring deviations from the security baseline is crucial. Any necessary exceptions, such as open ports required for specific applications, should be clearly documented for future reference and troubleshooting.

The dynamic nature of the threat landscape means that continuous vigilance is essential. Administrators must ensure that any changes to the configuration adhere strictly to approved policies and undergo formal change control processes. Often, unauthorized adjustments are made under pressure to resolve immediate operational issues, which can unintentionally introduce security risks.

Configuration management is a lifecycle process. From the initial hardening of a newly acquired system to the ongoing monitoring and adjustment of its configuration, every step is critical. Automated processes can significantly reduce human error, ensuring that security measures are comprehensively and consistently applied. By understanding and implementing vital configuration management practices, we not only safeguard our systems but also streamline troubleshooting and maintenance, ensuring a secure and efficient operational environment.

5.2 Patch Management

Patch management is the foundation of network security, aimed at ensuring all devices within a network are secure. This process is critical, as exemplified by the infamous Equifax breach, where a failure to apply a timely patch led to significant data exposure.

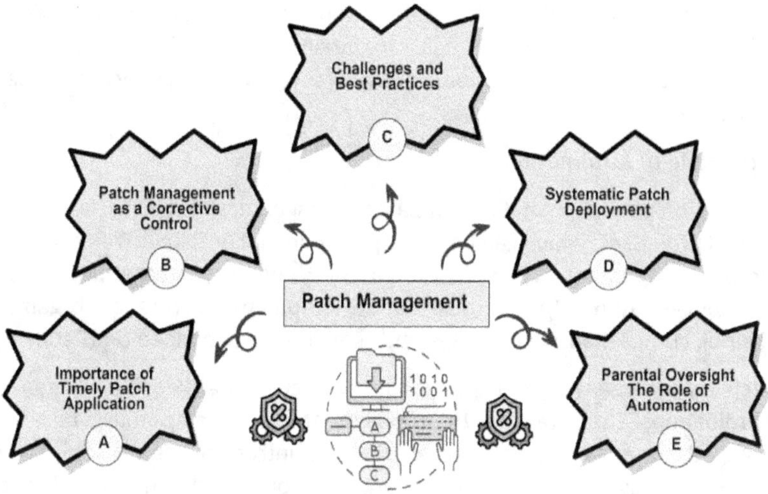

A) Importance of Timely Patch Application

The Equifax incident underscores a critical vulnerability: once a patch is released, attackers are also aware of the underlying security weakness. Hence, it is crucial to test patches in a controlled environment before deploying them to production. This process must be quick and efficient, as delays can lead to severe consequences, as seen with Equifax, who had the patch available for two months without applying it.

B) Patch Management as a Corrective Control

Patch management functions as a corrective control that addresses vulnerabilities. Software developers are expected to release patches for known issues, which should be applied regularly. For instance, Microsoft adheres to a predictable schedule known as "Patch Tuesday," providing a routine for updates that allows organizations to plan their patch testing and deployment.

C) Challenges and Best Practices

Despite the existence of patches, the application can sometimes be complicated. Administrators must balance the need to fix vulnerabilities with the potential for new patches to disrupt system functionality. This requires a detailed testing phase where patches are evaluated for stability and compatibility before full deployment.

The protocol after "Patch Tuesday" involves a waiting period—typically one to two weeks—to monitor community feedback and test the patch internally. This cautious approach helps avoid the introduction of new issues into the production environment.

D) Systematic Patch Deployment

Patch management should be integrated into the broader change management process to ensure that all modifications are thoroughly reviewed and documented. This integration helps maintain a record of changes, provides a clear audit trail, and ensures consistency in security practices across all devices, not just servers.

E) The Role of Automation

Automation plays a pivotal role in patch management, reducing the reliance on manual processes, which can be error-prone and inconsistent. Tools like System Center Configuration Manager (SCCM) or Windows Server Update Services (WSUS) can automate the distribution of patches across an organization, ensuring comprehensive coverage and reducing the workload on IT staff.

Patch management is a critical security practice that requires diligence and coordination. From testing to deployment, every step must be carefully managed to ensure that patches do not introduce new problems while addressing existing vulnerabilities. Organizations must strive for a balanced approach that prioritizes security without compromising system stability.

5.3 Change Management

Change management is a crucial process within IT and cybersecurity. It provides a formalized approach to handling all modifications within an organization's environment. This section will discuss the systematic approach required to manage changes effectively, ensuring stability and security across all operations.

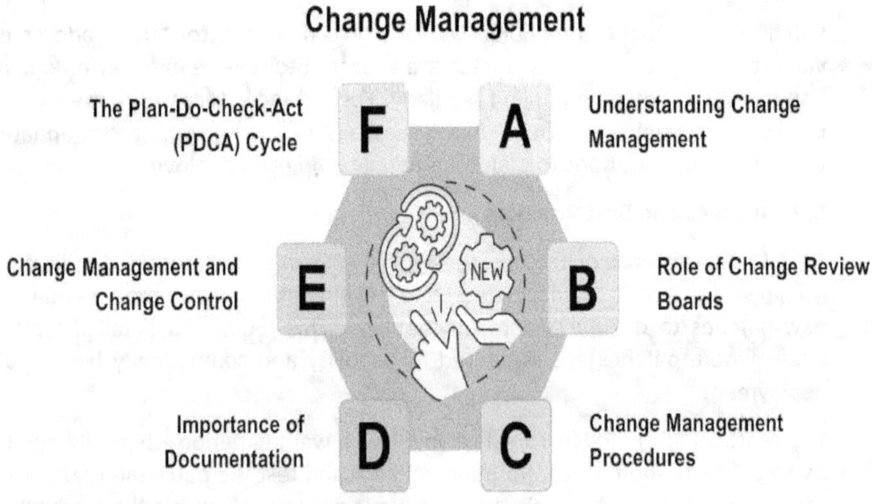

A) Understanding Change Management

Change management encompasses everything from minor updates to significant system changes. It involves a systematic process where every change, whether it is applying patches, upgrading systems, or configuring network devices, must be thoroughly reviewed and justified. The process ensures that all potential impacts are considered and managed before changes are implemented.

B) The Role of Change Review Boards

At the heart of the change management process is the Change Review Board (CRB), composed of IT professionals and operational stakeholders directly impacted by the changes. This board, along with any necessary sub-boards such as Technical Approval Boards, evaluates and approves all proposed changes. Their goal is to ensure that every change serves a beneficial purpose without introducing undue risk.

For instance, when updating critical systems like a pharmacy server, it is crucial to involve representatives from the pharmacy department. They can provide insights into how proposed changes might affect their operations and help in translating technical details into operational impacts, ensuring that all parties understand the implications.

C) Change Management Procedures

The general flow of change management begins with identifying the need for change. This is followed by a detailed proposal that outlines the reasons, impacts, potential benefits, and risks associated with the change. Once the proposal is provisionally approved, the change undergoes testing in a controlled environment to confirm its effectiveness and safety.

If the test results are favorable, the change is formally scheduled and communicated to all affected parties, ensuring everyone is prepared for any associated downtime or adjustments. The implementation phase is closely monitored, followed by post-implementation reviews to assess the change's success and gather lessons learned for future changes.

D) Importance of Documentation

Documentation plays a critical role throughout the change management process. Comprehensive records are vital for auditing purposes and provide valuable references for future modifications. They help maintain continuity and understanding, especially when original team members are no longer available.

E) Differentiating Change Management and Change Control

It is essential to distinguish between change management and change control. While change management refers to the fundamental process encompassing all stages of a change, change control focuses specifically on the phases where changes are being actively implemented and controlled to ensure they align with the planned outcomes.

F) The PDCA Cycle

The Plan-Do-Check-Act (PDCA) cycle is a fundamental concept in change management. It emphasizes the continuous nature of managing changes. This cycle helps organizations continuously improve their change processes by planning changes, implementing them, monitoring the outcomes, and adjusting as necessary before starting the cycle anew.

This section covered the integral components of change management, highlighting the importance of a structured approach to managing changes in IT environments. Through rigid planning, testing, and documentation, organizations can ensure that changes enhance system functionality without compromising security or stability.

5.4 Introduction to Cryptography

Cryptography is the science of securing communication. It plays a crucial role in the confidentiality, integrity, authentication, and non-repudiation of information. As we discuss this deeply, we start with a historical perspective, not only to appreciate its evolution and relevance but also because understanding the origins of cryptographic methods will help in understanding modern practices, which is essential for technological development.

A) Historical Context and Symmetric Encryption

Our journey begins with the Spartan Scytale, an early form of symmetric encryption, which involved wrapping a piece of parchment around a stick of a specific diameter to write a message. Only with a stick of the same diameter could the recipient rewrap the parchment and read the message correctly. This method illustrates the use of a shared secret or critical in symmetric encryption, where both the sender and the receiver use the same key for encryption and decryption.

B) Difference between Symmetric and Asymmetric Encryption

In cryptography, encryption methodologies can broadly be categorized into two types: symmetric and asymmetric encryption. Each type serves unique purposes and has its strengths and weaknesses. Understanding these can help in selecting the appropriate encryption method depending on the security requirements and context.

C) Symmetric Encryption

Definition and Mechanics: Symmetric encryption, also known as secret key encryption, involves a single key that both the sender and the recipient use to encrypt and decrypt messages. This key must be kept secret and shared securely between parties before communication can commence.

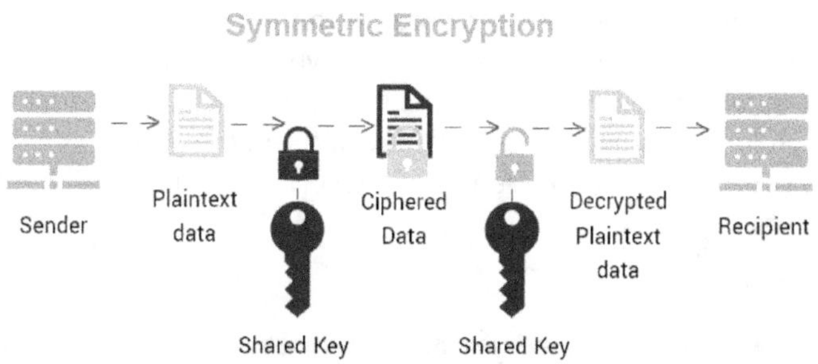

Advantages:

- **Speed:** Symmetric encryption algorithms are generally faster and less computationally intensive than their asymmetric counterparts, making them suitable for encrypting large volumes of data.
- **Simplicity:** The process involves only one key, making the mechanism more straightforward in terms of key management, provided the key is securely shared and stored.

Disadvantages:

- **Critical Distribution Problem:** The major drawback is the requirement to distribute the key securely to all parties without interception. If a third party obtains the key, they can decrypt all messages encrypted with that key.
- **Scalability:** As the number of participants in a network grows, the secure distribution of keys becomes more complex and challenging.

D) Asymmetric Encryption

Definition and Mechanics: Asymmetric encryption, also known as public key encryption, utilizes a pair of keys—a public key and a private key. The public key is shared openly to encrypt messages, while the private key is kept secret by the owner and used to decrypt messages.

Advantages:

- **Security in Key Distribution:** The public key can be distributed openly without compromising security, as only the corresponding private key can decrypt messages encrypted with the public key. This resolves the critical distribution problem seen in symmetric encryption.

- **Digital Signatures:** Asymmetric encryption facilitates digital signatures, where a message can be signed with a sender's private key and verified by others using the sender's public key, ensuring authenticity and integrity.

Disadvantages:

- **Speed and Resource Intensity:** Asymmetric algorithms are slower and require more computational resources due to the complexity of the math involved, which can be a disadvantage for encrypting large amounts of data.
- **Key Size and Management:** The keys used in asymmetric encryption are typically longer, and managing these keys, especially the secure storage of private keys, poses its challenges.

E) The Caesar Cipher

Moving forward, we explore the Caesar Cipher, a substitution cipher that shifts the letters of the plaintext a certain number of places down or up the alphabet. For example, shifting the letters three places to the left transforms the phrase "pass the exam" into "MXPP QEB BUXJ". This simple yet effective technique underpins many modern cryptographic algorithms.

F) The Role of Cryptography in Security

Cryptography's primary role is to maintain the secrecy of digital communications, but its utility spans beyond just confidentiality. It ensures the integrity of information, authenticates the identity of parties in communication, and provides mechanisms for non-repudiation.

Understanding Terminologies

- **Cryptology:** The broader science of secure communication.
- **Cryptography:** Specifically involves creating messages with hidden meanings.
- **Cryptanalysis:** Refers to the methods of breaking encrypted communications, where the attacker may use mathematical analysis or side-channel attacks to exploit vulnerabilities in the implementation rather than attempting to break a robust algorithm directly.
- **Cipher:** The specific algorithm used for encryption and decryption.
- **Plaintext:** The original, readable message.
- **Ciphertext:** The encrypted message is only readable with the correct key.

G) Encryption Types

- **Book Cipher:** Uses a common book as a key where messages are encoded through page and word references.
- **Running-Key Cipher:** Employs a repeating text or phrase as a key to encode a message.

H) The Essence of Cipher Algorithms

A cipher is the algorithmic backbone of cryptography, responsible for transforming plaintext into ciphertext and ciphertext into plaintext. This transformation is central to securing sensitive or confidential data.

I) Legacy Encryption Techniques

While modern encryption techniques are sophisticated and powerful, understanding legacy methods like the Book Cipher and Running-Key Cipher provides insight into the evolution of cryptographic practices. These methods used simple but innovative techniques for encoding messages, relying on a shared secret book or phrase to encrypt and decrypt information.

This section sets the stage for a deeper exploration of the various types of encryption and their applications in securing modern communications. As we continue, remember that the goal is to achieve a balance between confidentiality and availability, ensuring that encryption is strong enough to prevent attacks but not so unmanageable as to restrict legitimate access to information.

5.4.1 Asymmetric Encryption

Although asymmetric encryption is a relatively recent technique compared to millennia-old symmetric encryption, it is essential in modern secure communications. Invented in the 1970s with renowned algorithms such as Diffie-Hellman and Rivest-Shamir-Adleman (RSA), it revolutionized data protection, especially over public and insecure networks like the Internet. For example, asymmetric encryption is commonly used in securing email communications through protocols like S/MIME and encrypting data exchanged during online banking transactions.

Final Cyber Security Compass Assessment:

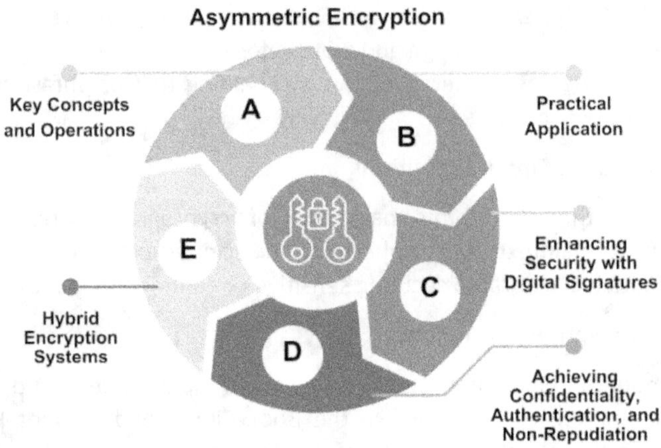

A) Key Concepts and Operations

Asymmetric encryption requires a pair of keys for each user: a public key, which is openly shared and used for encrypting messages, and a private key, which is kept secret and used for decrypting messages. This key pair mechanism ensures that anyone can send a secure message to the receiver, but only the receiver can decrypt it with their private key, thus maintaining confidentiality.

B) Practical Application

In practical terms, if Alice wants to send a confidential message to Bob, she will encrypt her message using Bob's public key. Only Bob can decrypt this message using his private key. This method addresses the fundamental challenge of symmetric encryption, which requires a secure method to share the secret key beforehand.

C) Enhancing Security with Digital Signatures

Beyond confidentiality, asymmetric encryption is crucial for authentication and non-repudiation through digital signatures. By encrypting a message with her private key, Alice can provide proof that the message came from her, as anyone with her public key can verify this. This method, however, does not ensure confidentiality but confirms the sender's identity and that the message has not been altered.

D) Achieving Confidentiality, Authentication, and Non-Repudiation

To achieve both confidentiality and authentication, the message can be encrypted twice: once with Alice's private key for authentication and then with Bob's public key for confidentiality. This dual encryption ensures that the message comes from Alice and that only Bob can read it.

E) Hybrid Encryption Systems

In reality, the use of pure asymmetric encryption is limited due to its computational intensity. Instead, hybrid systems are commonly used, where asymmetric encryption secures the key exchange for a faster symmetric encryption system that handles the actual data transmission. This approach combines the strengths of both encryption types—security in crucial distribution and efficiency in data transfer.

Understanding asymmetric encryption is crucial for anyone involved in securing digital communications. Its ability to facilitate secure key exchange over an insecure medium and provide digital signatures for authentication makes it an integral part of modern cryptography.

5.4.2 Understanding Hashing in Cryptography

Hashing is a fundamental concept in cryptography, utilized primarily for verifying the integrity of data. Unlike other cryptographic methods, hashing is a one-way function, meaning once data is transformed into a hash, it cannot be reversed back to the original form. This unique property makes hashing an invaluable tool for ensuring that data remains unchanged and untampered.

Understanding Hashing in Cryptography

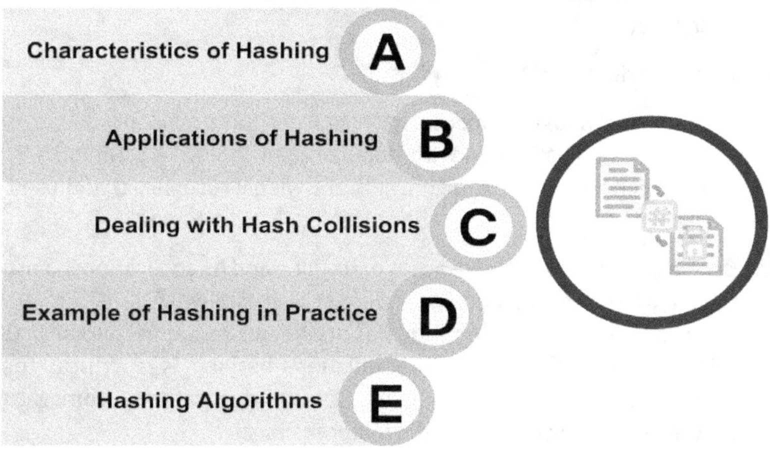

A) Characteristics of Hashing

A key aspect of hashing is its ability to take variable-length plaintext and convert it into a fixed-length hash, often referred to as a Message Digest (MD). Regardless of the input size—whether it is a few characters or extensive documents—the output will always be of a constant length specified by the hash function used.

B) Applications of Hashing

The primary use of hashing is to verify data integrity. Common scenarios include:

- **Software downloads:** Hash values are often provided alongside downloadable files. By hashing the downloaded file and comparing it with the provided hash, users can verify whether the file has been altered from its original state.
- **Digital forensics:** Hashing is crucial in forensic analysis, particularly when verifying the integrity of data on storage devices. Investigators hash drives and their copies to ensure that the digital evidence has not been altered during the forensic process.

C) Dealing with Hash Collisions

A collision occurs when two different inputs produce the same hash output. Although rare, collisions are significant because they can undermine the hash's reliability in proving data integrity. The likelihood of collisions depends on the robustness of the hash function used.

D) Example of Hashing in Practice

To illustrate, consider hashing the first chapter of Charles Dickens's "Great Expectations." Initially, the chapter is hashed to produce a specific digest. Altering just a single comma in the text results in a completely different hash, demonstrating how sensitive hash functions are to input changes. This sensitivity ensures that even minor alterations to the data are detectable through changes in the hash value.

E) Hashing Algorithms

While detailed knowledge of specific hashing algorithms may only be necessary for some exams, familiarization with popular algorithms like MD5, SHA-2, and SHA-3 can be beneficial. These algorithms are widely recognized and used due to their reliability and the security they offer against tampering.

In this section, we explored the concept of hashing and its application in ensuring data integrity. Hashing functions provide a secure, one-way transformation of data that helps verify that information has not been altered. Despite its inability to provide confidentiality or non-repudiation, hashing is a critical tool in maintaining the integrity of data across various applications, from securing software downloads to conducting digital forensics.

5.4.3 Cryptographic Attacks

In this section, we will explore various attacks on the cryptographic systems protecting our data. Understanding these attacks helps devise effective security measures and strategies to defend against them.

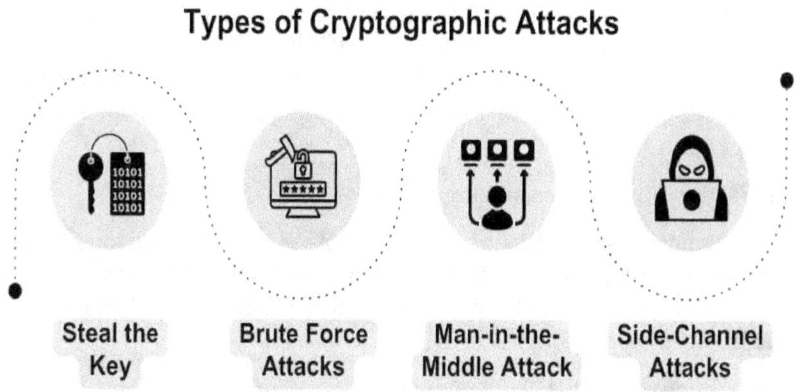

A) Types of Cryptographic Attacks

1. **Steal the Key:** The most straightforward and often most effective attack on cryptography is to steal the encryption keys. Instead of breaking the encryption, which can be computationally intensive and time-consuming, attackers often target the keys stored on systems. This method is direct and bypasses the need to crack the encryption algorithms.
2. **Brute Force Attacks:** Brute force attacks involve trying every possible combination to decrypt the encrypted data. This method is straightforward but requires significant time and computing resources, making it impractical against solid encryption standards. However, brute force remains a theoretical threat to any encrypted system.
3. **Man-in-the-Middle (MITM) Attack:** In an MITM attack, the attacker intercepts communications between two parties without their knowledge, relaying and possibly altering the data. For example, if Bob sends John a message, Mike could intercept and modify the communication without either party knowing. Effective use of encryption and secure communication protocols can mitigate this risk.
4. **Side-Channel Attacks:** These attacks involve gaining insights into the encryption process by analyzing information from the physical system, such as power consumption or processing time. Such attacks exploit weaknesses in system implementation rather than the cryptographic algorithms themselves.

B) Countermeasures and Security Enhancements

To defend against these attacks, several strategies can be employed:

1. **For Steal the Key:** Ensure that encryption keys are stored securely using hardware security modules or other secure storage solutions.
2. **For Brute Force:** Implement rate-limiting and account lockout mechanisms to prevent repeated guessing attempts. Additionally, use essential stretching techniques to increase the time required to test each key.

3. **For MITM Attacks:** Utilize end-to-end encryption and secure protocols like HTTPS to ensure data integrity and authenticity.
4. **For Side-Channel Attacks:** Design systems to minimize leakage of operational information and use randomized processing techniques to hide patterns.

C) Practical Applications and Implications

Understanding and anticipating these attacks is crucial for anyone involved in securing sensitive data. By studying these methods, professionals can better prepare and implement strategies that ensure the confidentiality, integrity, and availability of information.

This section covered the fundamental attacks on cryptographic systems and discussed practical measures to protect against them. As we continue to rely more on digital communications, the importance of vital cryptographic practices cannot be overstated. By staying informed about potential vulnerabilities and countermeasures, we can safeguard our data against these evolving threats.

5.5 Data Handling, Storage, and Retention

This section discusses the critical aspects of Data Handling, Storage, and Retention, which are crucial for safeguarding information throughout its lifecycle. Understanding these processes is essential for ensuring data integrity, confidentiality, and availability in accordance with regulatory requirements and organizational policies.

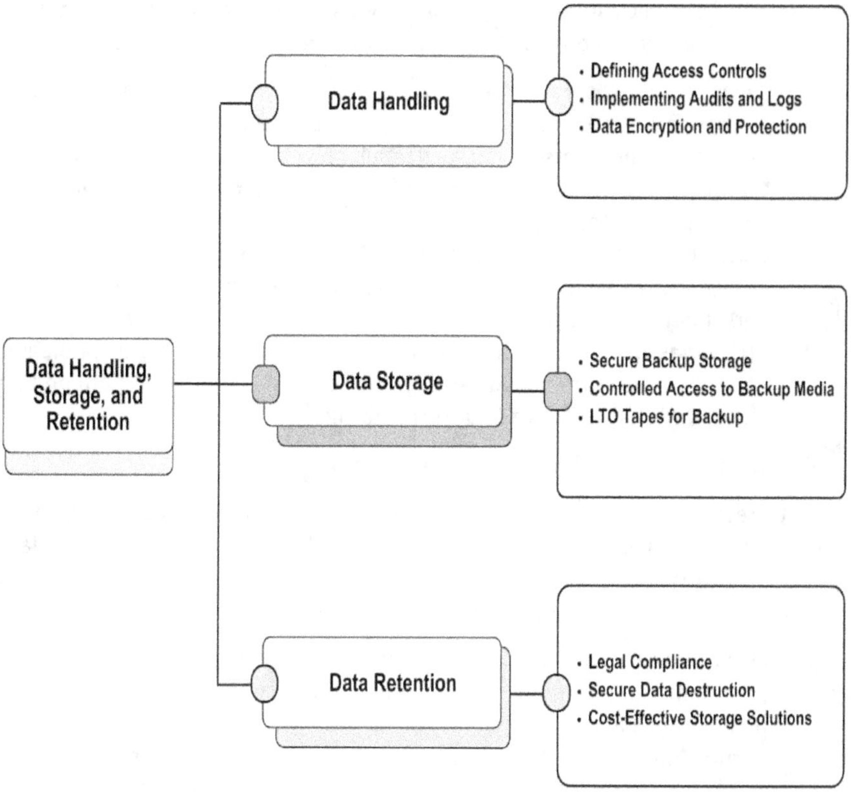

A) Data Handling

Data handling involves managing how data is accessed and used within an organization. It encompasses setting vital policies to ensure that only authorized personnel have access to sensitive data strictly on a need-to-know basis. Effective data handling requires:

1. **Defining Access Controls:** Establish clear policies on who can access data and specific conditions under which access is granted.
2. **Implementing Audits and Logs:** Maintaining comprehensive audit trails and logging systems to monitor and verify legitimate data access, enhancing accountability and traceability.
3. **Data Encryption and Protection:** All sensitive data should be keyed in as encrypted at rest and during transit so that no unauthorized people can tamper with the data stored. Data masking, tokenization, and regular backups protect data from breaches, loss, or fraudulent manipulation.

B) Data Storage

The physical and digital storage of data requires strict security measures to prevent unauthorized access and ensure data availability, especially in disaster scenarios. The security of data storage is vital, as attackers often target weakly protected data repositories. Key practices include:

1. **Secure Backup Storage:** Utilizing geographically distant, climate-controlled storage facilities to safeguard backup tapes, ensuring they are not affected by localized disasters. This practice aligns with maintaining an acceptable Maximum Tolerable Downtime (MTD), which dictates how quickly data needs to be restored.
2. **Controlled Access to Backup Media:** Physical access to backup tapes must be strictly controlled, with measures like requiring ID verification for personnel handling sensitive data.
3. **LTO Tapes for Backup:** Employing Linear Tape-Open (LTO) technology for backups, which offers high capacity (up to 30TB compressed data on LTO-8 tapes) and cost-effective long-term storage.

C) Data Retention

Data retention policies dictate how long data should be kept based on legal requirements and business needs. These policies must balance regulatory compliance with practical storage considerations, especially for organizations dealing with large volumes of data. Key considerations include:

1. **Legal Compliance:** Adhering to industry-specific regulations that mandate minimum retention periods for critical data, such as financial records or health information.
2. **Secure Data Destruction:** Once the retention period expires, data must be securely destroyed to prevent unauthorized access or breaches.
3. **Cost-Effective Storage Solutions:** Employing cost-effective solutions like tape storage, which offers high capacity at a lower cost, for long-term data retention.

D) Practical Implementation

Real-world implementation of these policies includes:

1. **Disaster Recovery Planning:** Integrating data storage and retention strategies into broader disaster recovery plans, ensuring that data can be restored quickly and efficiently after a disruption.
2. **Periodic Reviews:** Regularly reviewing data handling, storage, and retention policies to adapt to changing regulations and business needs.
3. **Employee Training:** Educating employees on the importance of data security and their roles in maintaining it.

Understanding and implementing effective data handling, storage, and retention strategies are crucial for protecting an organization's data integrity and legal compliance. This section aims to equip you with the knowledge to develop policies and practices that ensure strong data management and security in your professional roles.

5.6 Data Disposal - Ensuring Secure Destruction of Sensitive Information

Secure data disposal is a crucial step in the lifecycle of data management. It ensures that sensitive information does not fall into the wrong hands. This section will focus on the methods and best practices for securely disposing of data, particularly magnetic backup tapes that have reached the end of their retention period.

A) Understanding the Importance of Secure Disposal

Improper data disposal can lead to significant security risks, including data breaches and identity theft. As such, it is vital to implement strict data disposal processes to eliminate potential vulnerabilities.

B) Disposal of Backup Tapes

Once the retention period expires and there is no further use for the data, secure disposal methods must be employed. Here are the steps and considerations for disposing of backup tapes:

1. **Verification of Data Redundancy:** Ensure that all necessary data has been securely transferred or backed up elsewhere before proceeding with disposal.
2. **Selection of Disposal Methods:** Choose an appropriate disposal method that complies with industry standards and legal requirements. Common methods include:
   - **Physical Destruction:** Industrial shredders or crushers are designed to destroy the tape physically, making data recovery impossible.
   - **Degaussing:** Employing a degausser to disrupt the magnetic fields on the tape, effectively erasing the data.
   - **Crypto Shredding**: Encrypting data before disposal and then securely deleting or destroying the encryption keys, rendering the data unreadable even if residual data remains.
   - **Cloud Data Sanitization:** In cloud environments, utilizing provider-specific data destruction services such as cryptographic erasure or secure wipe protocols to ensure data is irrecoverable after decommissioning.
3. **Vendor Selection for Disposal Services:** If using a third-party service for data destruction, ensure the vendor is licensed and bonded. Verify their credentials and track record for compliance with security standards.
4. **Documentation and Verification:** Maintain a chain of custody and obtain certificates of destruction from the vendor to document the secure disposal of the tapes. This serves as proof of compliance with data protection

regulations. In addition to these methods, regularly reviewing disposal procedures and maintaining documentation ensures compliance and enhances data security during disposal processes.

C) Best Practices for Secure Data Disposal

1. **Cross-Shredding Paper Data:** For any sensitive information on paper, utilize cross-cut shredders that cut both horizontally and vertically, significantly reducing the risk of data reconstruction.
2. **Implementing Access Controls:** Ensure that only authorized personnel have access to data disposal facilities and that all interactions are logged and monitored.
3. **Regular Audits:** Conduct regular audits of disposal procedures to ensure compliance with policies and to identify any potential improvements.

The secure disposal of data is a critical component of data security. By understanding the appropriate methods and implementing strict controls, organizations can protect themselves from the risks associated with data leakage. This section aims to equip you with the knowledge to manage the disposal of sensitive data effectively, ensuring it is done safely and in compliance with all relevant regulations.

5.7 Understanding Directive or Administrative Controls

This section discusses the Directive or Administrative Controls within an organization's security framework. These controls encompass policies, procedures, and educational measures that guide personnel behavior and system operation.

A) The Role of Administrative Controls

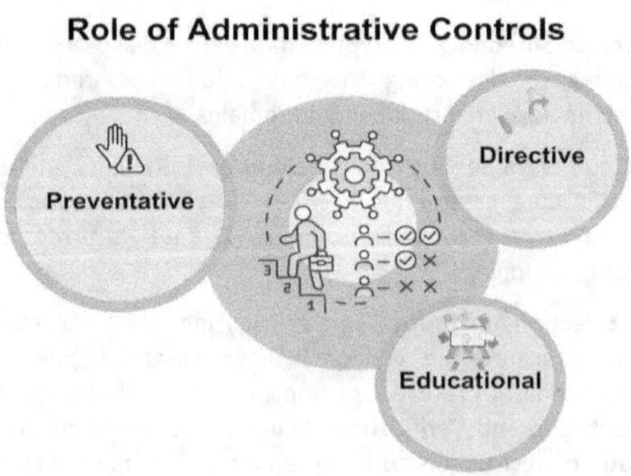

Administrative controls form the backbone of an organization's security protocols, defining how data should be handled, accessed, and protected. These controls are:

1. **Preventative:** Aimed at preventing security breaches through clear guidelines.
2. **Directive:** Provide directions on implementing technical and physical security measures.
3. **Educational:** Focus on training employees to adhere to security protocols and understand the importance of compliance.

B) Coordination with Technical and Physical Controls

While administrative controls provide the framework and intent, they must be supported by:

1. **Technical Controls:** Such as encryption and firewalls, which provide the mechanisms to protect data electronically.
2. **Physical Controls:** Including locks and access cards, which secure physical assets and locations.

C) Access Control Types

In implementing administrative controls, it is essential to understand the various types of access controls:

1. **Preventative Controls:** Designed to prevent unauthorized access or breaches.
2. **Detective Controls:** Identify and alert the occurrence of a security incident.
3. **Corrective Controls:** Address and rectify security breaches.
4. **Recovery Controls:** Enable the restoration of operations and systems after a breach.
5. **Deterrent Controls:** Discourage security violations that could be harmful towards an organization.
6. **Compensating Controls:** Provide alternative security measures when standard controls cannot be applied.

D) Developing and Implementing Policies

Effective security policies are crucial for maintaining an organization's security posture:

1. **Policy Development:** Policies should be developed based on the organization's values, vision, and business objectives. They should be comprehensive but understandable, outlining clear and actionable guidelines for all employees.
2. **Approval and Maintenance:** Policies require regular updates to ensure they remain relevant and practical in light of changing technologies and external regulations.

3. **Training and Compliance:** Continuous employee education on these policies is crucial to ensuring compliance and adapting to evolving security challenges.

E) Example Policies in Cybersecurity

Several key policies typically govern IT and cybersecurity practices within organizations:

1. **Acceptable Use Policy:** Defines what is considered acceptable use of the organization's networks and devices.
2. **BYOD (Bring Your Device) Policy:** This policy outlines the protocols for employees who wish to use personal devices for work purposes, ensuring that these devices do not compromise the organization's security.
3. **Password Policy:** Specifies requirements for creating and maintaining secure passwords, such as complexity requirements and change intervals.
4. **Data Handling Policy:** Details procedures for managing, storing, and destroying data securely to ensure confidentiality and integrity.

Directive or Administrative Controls are essential for establishing a security-conscious culture within an organization. By setting the standards and expectations for security, these controls enable a systematic approach to protecting sensitive information and assets. This section aims to provide a comprehensive understanding of how these controls integrate with technical and physical measures to secure an organization effectively.

5.8 Enhancing Security through Training and Awareness

This section explores the critical role of training and awareness in reinforcing an organization's security framework. While users are often viewed as an organization's greatest asset, without proper education, they can also pose significant security risks.

A) Importance of Training and Awareness

Practical training and awareness programs are essential to mitigate risks associated with human error, which is often non-malicious but potentially devastating. The primary objectives of these programs are to:

1. **Educate Users:** Equip employees with the necessary knowledge to handle data securely and recognize security threats.
2. **Change Behaviors:** Shift employee habits through continuous engagement and reinforcement of security best practices.
3. **Encourage a Security-Conscious Culture:** Develop an environment where security considerations are integrated into daily activities.

B) Methods of Effective Training

To ensure training is practical and engaging, it should include:

1. **Interactive Sessions:** Move away from boring presentations to more interactive, discussion-based sessions.
2. **Gamification:** Incorporate game-like elements to make learning about security fun and engaging. This can include rewards for compliance and recognition for proactive security behaviors.
3. **Regular Refreshers:** Implement regular training sessions to keep security top of mind and address new threats.

C) Implementation Strategies

1. **Top-Down Support:** Secure commitment from senior management to provide the necessary resources for comprehensive training programs.

2. **Role-Specific Training:** Design training sessions to the specific needs and risks associated with different roles within the organization.
3. **Security Champions:** Appoint security champions within teams to promote security awareness and practices among users.

D) Rewards and Recognition

Utilizing motivations can significantly enhance engagement in security training:

1. **Immediate Rewards:** Offer immediate rewards for correct answers or behaviors during training sessions to reinforce learning.
2. **Long-Term Incentives:** Implement ongoing competitions or recognition programs that reward long-term compliance and vigilance, such as recognizing the best-performing team in handling phishing attempts.

E) Security Training as an Administrative Control

Training and awareness are considered administrative or directive controls within the security policy framework. They are foundational to:

1. **Guiding the Design of Technical Controls:** Inform the development of technical security measures by providing insights into potential human factors that could impact security.
2. **Complementing Physical Controls:** Work alongside physical security measures to ensure a comprehensive defense strategy.

F) Example Scenario: Phishing Awareness

A practical application of training effectiveness can be illustrated through a phishing awareness program:

1. **Scenario-Based Training:** Conduct training that simulates phishing attacks to teach employees how to recognize and respond to them.
2. **Post-Training Evaluation:** After training, send a mock phishing email to measure the response rate and effectiveness of the training.
3. **Recognition and Rewards:** Reward departments or individuals with the highest reporting rates to encourage ongoing vigilance against phishing.

Training and awareness are essential components of an organization's security strategy. By educating employees and continuously engaging them in security practices, organizations can significantly reduce the risk of breaches and enhance their overall security posture. This section underscores the necessity of investing in effective training programs that not only inform but also motivate employees to be proactive in their security practices.

5.9 Understanding Social Engineering

This section explores the vital concept of Social Engineering within cybersecurity. Often exploited by malicious actors and essential for penetration testers conducting simulated attacks, social engineering focuses on manipulating the human element—typically considered the weakest link in security defenses. For example, attackers might craft convincing phishing emails that appear to come from trusted sources, such as a company's finance team, to trick employees into revealing sensitive information or clicking malicious links.

A) Concept and Execution

Social engineering involves manipulating individuals into breaking security protocols to gain unauthorized access to systems or data. This low-tech strategy can bypass even the most powerful technical defenses by exploiting human psychology rather than relying on sophisticated hacking techniques.

B) Importance of Comprehensive Security

While organizations may invest heavily in perimeter defenses, the lack of depth in internal security layers can leave them vulnerable. The principle of "zero trust"—never trust, always verify—is essential in mitigating such vulnerabilities. It requires vital authentication processes each time a resource is accessed.

C) Techniques in Social Engineering

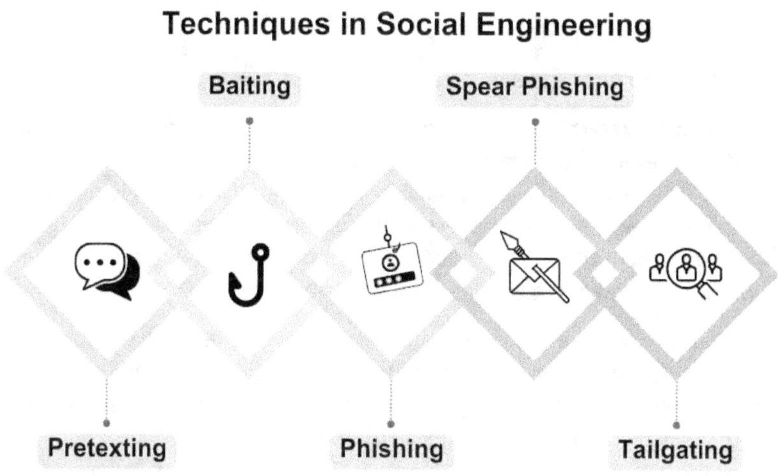

1. **Pretexting:** Attackers create a fabricated scenario to obtain personal information. Common pretexts include posing as IT staff needing credentials to resolve a fictitious issue.
2. **Baiting:** Similar to pretexting, baiting involves offering something enticing to the victim, such as free software download, to steal their data.
3. **Phishing:** This involves sending fraudulent communications that appear to come from reputable sources to steal sensitive data like credit card numbers and login information.
4. **Spear Phishing:** Unlike phishing, which targets large groups, spear phishing targets specific individuals or organizations.

5. **Tailgating:** An attacker seeking entry to a restricted area follows an authorized person into a building.

D) The Ice Cream Truck Experiment

A notable example of social engineering involved a penetration testing firm that set up an "Employee Appreciation Day" with a fake ice cream truck. Employees were offered free ice cream in exchange for their usernames and passwords, demonstrating the alarming effectiveness of such tactics. An astounding 95% of employees provided their credentials for free ice cream.

E) Strategies for Counteracting Social Engineering

1. **Education and Awareness:** Regular training sessions should be conducted to educate employees about the risks of social engineering and how to recognize its signs.
2. **Simulated Attacks:** Organizations can conduct controlled social engineering attacks to test their employee's vigilance and the effectiveness of their training programs.
3. **Policy Enforcement:** Implement strict policies regarding information sharing and ensure they are followed through regular audits and reinforcement.

F) Implementing a Zero Trust Model

Adopting a zero trust model involves:

1. **Verifying Everything:** Every request for access to resources must be authenticated, authorized, and continuously validated.
2. **Least Privilege:** Apply the principle of least privilege by giving users the minimum level of access necessary to perform their jobs.
3. **Microsegmentation:** Use microsegmentation to limit lateral movement within the network in case an attacker gains access.

Social engineering poses a significant threat due to its reliance on human error rather than technological vulnerabilities. Organizations can mitigate the risks posed by social engineering tactics by understanding and implementing vital security practices, training, and a zero-trust model.

5.10 Understanding Phishing

Phishing, with a 'PH', is a method of cyber deception aimed at obtaining sensitive information through fraudulent means. This section explores various phishing techniques, such as spear phishing, whale phishing, vishing (voice phishing), and smishing (SMS phishing), which are pivotal for both cybersecurity exams and real-world defences.

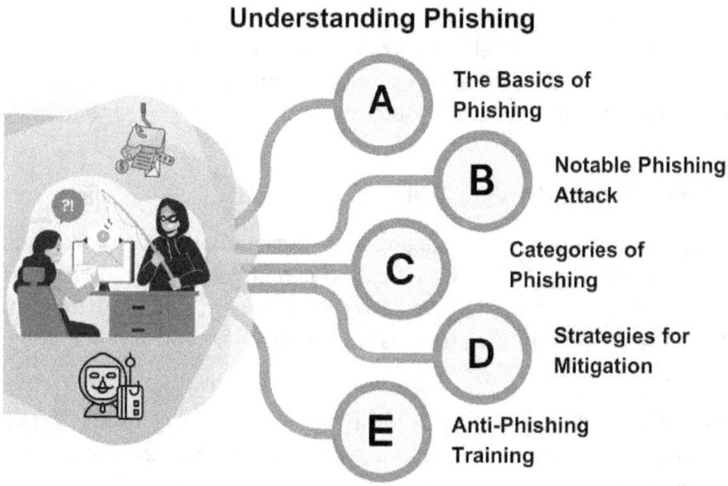

A) The Basics of Phishing

Phishing attacks typically involve emails that lure recipients into providing personal data, clicking on malicious links, or executing unsafe attachments. These emails often promise rewards ("Click here to claim your $50 Amazon card") or create urgency ("Confirm your account details or your account will be closed"). Despite their simplicity, these schemes can be remarkably effective at deceiving users.

B) Notable Phishing Attack

One striking example involved a public treasurer from Michigan who was deceived into sending $1.2 million to a scammer in Nigeria, believing he would receive a substantial inheritance. This incident underscores the significant risks associated with phishing and the importance of educating staff about these threats.

C) Categories of Phishing:

1. **Regular Phishing:** Casts a wide net by sending out massive numbers of emails, aiming for a few responses.
2. **Spear Phishing:** Involves targeted emails designed to trick specific individuals by using information tailored specifically to them, increasing the likelihood of success.
3. **Whale Phishing:** Targets high-level executives (the 'big fish' or 'whales') with access to critical company areas. These attacks are highly customized and often involve considerable research.
4. **Vishing and Smishing:** Use voice calls and SMS texts, respectively, to deceive victims. Vishing might involve automated calls or live actors pretending to represent legitimate institutions, urging immediate action from the victim.

D) Strategies for Mitigation

Final Cyber Security Compass Assessment:

The most effective defense against phishing is comprehensive training and awareness programs that help employees recognize and respond appropriately to phishing attempts. Organizations should also employ technical measures such as email filtering, authentication protocols, and security layers that validate all communications.

E) Implementing Anti-Phishing Training

Training programs should be engaging and continuous, with regular updates to address new phishing tactics. Gamification can enhance learning outcomes by making the training process interactive and rewarding. Simulated phishing attacks can also help reinforce lessons and gauge employee vulnerability to real-world attacks.

Understanding the mechanisms of phishing and its various forms is crucial for both individuals and organizations to protect sensitive information and maintain cybersecurity. Practical training, combined with vital technical defences, forms the foundation of a comprehensive strategy to thwart these deceptive attacks.

Conclusion

As you reach the final pages of *Starting Career in Cybersecurity*, take a moment to reflect on the journey you've undertaken. This book was crafted to serve not as an endpoint, but as a compass — helping you navigate the many pathways that lie ahead in the dynamic world of Cybersecurity.

Throughout the chapters, you've explored the foundational Security Principles, the importance of Business Continuity, Disaster Recovery, and Incident Response, the critical role of Access Controls, the complexities of Network Security, and the operational excellence required in Security Operations. Along the way, you've been encouraged to think beyond technical mastery — to consider your values, leadership potential, and personal growth.

Cybersecurity is not a static field; it is a living, evolving discipline that demands continual learning and adaptability. New threats, technologies, and regulations emerge every day, challenging us to stay informed and resilient. But with curiosity, dedication, and a clear sense of purpose, you can not only thrive in this environment — you can help shape it.

Remember that every role, from entry-level analyst to CISO, contributes meaningfully to protecting the digital world. Your path may shift and evolve over time, and that is perfectly natural. Use the frameworks, concepts, and practical advice in this book to guide your decisions and fuel your ambition.

Finally, never underestimate the power of community and collaboration. The cybersecurity field thrives on shared knowledge and mutual support. Engage with peers, mentor others, and continue building relationships that enrich your professional journey.

This book may have provided a map, but the next steps are yours to take. Stay passionate, stay curious, and most importantly — stay secure.

I wish you success and fulfillment as you navigate your cybersecurity career.

Final Cyber Security Compass Assessment

At the end of this book, you can complete the final Cyber Security Compass Assessment.

Go back to the domain you read about and find the role that resonates with you.

Write down your desired future role, check the relevant domain in the appropriate section, and update your soft skills, hard skills, and motivation.

Keep in mind that other factors also play an important role in shaping your career.

Example:

Category	**Details**
Domain Name	Confidentiality
Future Role	Junior Security Analyst
Soft Skills	- Communication - Problem-Solving - Attention to Detail - Critical Thinking - Teamwork
Hard Skills	- Network Security - Risk Assessment - Incident Response - Security Tools and Technologies - Vulnerability Assessment
Value	- Integrity - Responsibility - Adaptability - Curiosity - Diligence
Motivation	- Professional Growth - Problem Solving - Making a Difference - Recognition - Continuous Learning
Result	You can use ATP resume scanners, qualitative, or quantitative scoring with numbers. Having the score

	above 50% gives you chances to start your career in Cybersecurity.

www.ingramcontent.com/pod-product-compliance
Lightning Source LLC
LaVergne TN
LVHW022048200926
848481LV00003B/837